NATIONAL GEOGRAPHIC
KiDS

PERSONALITY QUIZZES

TRACEY WEST

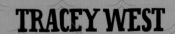

NATIONAL GEOGRAPHIC
Washington, D.C.

TABLE OF CONTENTS

Ready, Set, Quiz! 6

What's Your Shark Superpower?. . . . 8

Which Mountain Should
You Climb?. 10

Which Creepy-Crawly Critter
Are You?. 12

How Adventurous Are You?. 14

Which City Should You Live In?. . . 16

Which Dessert Are You?. 18

Choose: Make the Rules or
Break the Rules? 20

Which Bird of Prey Are You?. . . . 22

What's Your Galactic
Personality? 24

Are You a Dog or a Cat? 26

Would You Make a Good Pirate?. . . 28

Which Mythical Creature
Are You?. 30

Which Historical Fashion
Should You Rock?. 32

What Kind of Planet Protector
Are You?. 34

What Kind of Pet Should
You Get? 36

How Much of a Planner
Are You?. 38

What Type of Sci-Fi
Character Are You?. 40

Which Reptile Are You? 42

Choose: Thinking or Feeling?. . . 44

Which Ancient Greek God
Are You Most Like? 46

Which Oddball Animal Are You?. . . 48

Whose Artistic Spirit
Do You Share? 50

How Outgoing Are You? 52

Are You Ready for
an Adventure?. 54

Which Dinosaur Are You? 58

Could You Survive on
a Deserted Island? 60

Which Ocean Career Is for You? . . . 62

Which Australian Animal
Are You? 64

Which Ancient Civilization
Would You Have Fit Into? 66

Choose: Night Owl or
Early Bird? 68

Which Natural Wonder Should
You Visit? 70

How Silly Are You? 72

What Kind of Friend Are You? . . . 74

Which Gemstone Are You? 76

Are You More Like Thomas
Edison or Nikola Tesla? 78

How Will You Become Famous? . . . 80

Which Stinky Animal Are You? 82

How Curious Are You? 84

Which Animal Career Would
Be Best for You? 86

Who's Your Robot Sidekick? 88

Could You Have Survived
the Middle Ages? 90

What's Your Creative Strength? . . . 92

What's Your Historical
Leadership Style? 94

Are You Magical or Practical? . . . 96

What's Your Prey Power? 98

Are You a Perfectionist? 100

Which Awesome Sport
Should You Try? 102

Which Supercute Mammal
Are You? 104

What's Your Role on Mars? 106

Index 110

Which Ocean Career Is for You?

How Silly Are You?

Could You Survive on a Deserted Island?

Which Ancient Greek God Are You Most Like?

Which Dessert Are You?

Choose: Thinking or Feeling?

How Adventurous Are You?

Which Gemstone Are You?

READY, SET, QUIZ!

WHY DO PEOPLE LIKE TAKING PERSONALITY QUIZZES SO MUCH?

Maybe it's because we like learning about ourselves and what makes us special. Quizzes are an entertaining way to do that, but they're not always right, right? Have you ever gotten a quiz answer and said, "That's nothing like me at all!"? That's because quizzes aren't scientific—they're just for fun. So, if you don't like the answer you get, pick another one! It just shows that you did learn something about yourself, after all.

In this book you'll find quizzes about animals, adventure, exploring, times in history, and places all around the globe. Besides learning something new about yourself, you might learn some new things about the world, too.

INSIDE THIS BOOK YOU'LL FIND

5 DIFFERENT TYPES OF QUIZZES

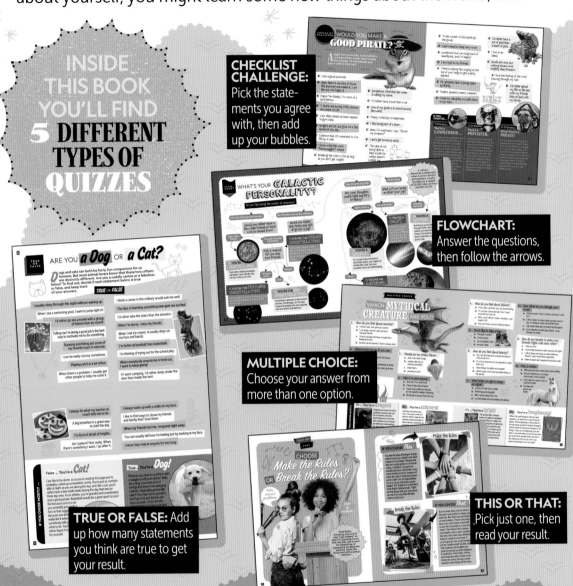

CHECKLIST CHALLENGE: Pick the statements you agree with, then add up your bubbles.

FLOWCHART: Answer the questions, then follow the arrows.

MULTIPLE CHOICE: Choose your answer from more than one option.

TRUE OR FALSE: Add up how many statements you think are true to get your result.

THIS OR THAT: Pick just one, then read your result.

TURN THE PAGE AND GET READY TO EXPLORE THE MOST UNIQUE PERSON IN THE UNIVERSE—YOU!

WHAT'S YOUR SHARK SUPERPOWER?

Sharks are some of the coolest creatures in the sea, thanks in part to their amazing abilities. How are you like a shark? Answer the questions to find out.

1. How do you get from one place to another?

a. I follow my instincts.
b. I ask for directions.
c. I travel in the shadows, where nobody can see me.
d. I run as fast as I can!

2. Choose a profession:

a. pilot
b. guitarist
c. martial arts instructor
d. professional athlete

3. Pick an item to bring while camping:

a. compass
b. walkie-talkie
c. camouflage jacket
d. new boots

4. When I'm in a group, other people ...

a. listen to my ideas.
b. ask me to play music on my phone.
c. don't really notice me.
d. can't keep up with me.

5. Choose an animal:

a. bat
b. stingray
c. trapdoor spider
d. cheetah

6. Every car should have ...

a. a GPS system.
b. satellite radio.
c. tinted windows.
d. a powerful engine.

7. **Pick a fashion accessory:**
   a. wristwatch
   b. headphones
   c. a black beanie
   d. running shoes

8. **When you're asleep, what do you dream about?**
   a. traveling the world
   b. searching for treasure
   c. being invisible
   d. winning a race

9. **Which of these is the most important?**
   a. knowledge
   b. food
   c. talent
   d. leadership

10. **Your friends always say you ...**
    a. know where you're going.
    b. are in tune with the world.
    c. are too quiet.
    d. are in a hurry.

IF YOU CHOSE MOSTLY ...

A's ... Long-distance navigation

You know how to get where you're going, just like tiger sharks, blue sharks, and hammerhead sharks. These sharks can swim in straight lines for miles and miles. How can they do that? Scientists think sharks can sense Earth's magnetic field. Tiny pores in the shark's snout allow the shark to detect the magnetic energy and follow it.

B's ... Supersensitivity to electricity

You are very in tune with the world around you, much like a shark in search of prey. Using the same specialized pores that help them navigate, sharks can detect weak electrical fields in the water. Any living creature in the water lets off an electric charge when its muscles contract. The sodium and

chlorine in seawater conducts this electricity. When sharks sense a charge, they can follow it straight to a tasty meal.

C's ... Ninja-like Stealth

You know how to blend into the background when you don't want to be noticed. This is a trait that sharks rely on. Underwater, sharks will quickly sneak up behind prey and ambush them before the prey can swim away. While sharks need speed and stealth to do this, the large, slow-moving Greenland shark has ninja-like skills, too. It finds seals sleeping beneath the water's surface to avoid polar bears and then sneaks up behind them and gobbles them down.

D's ... Super Speed

You love to do everything fast! The fastest shark, the shortfin mako shark, can swim after its prey at a speed of 45 miles an hour (72 km/h), and even reach a top speed of 50 miles an hour (80 km/h) for short periods of time. That's much faster than a human can move—Olympian runner Usain Bolt's record-breaking speed is 27 miles an hour (43 km/h).

WHICH MOUNTAIN SHOULD YOU CLIMB?

Expert mountain climbers train before scaling peaks. How long would you be willing to train before you explore?

At least a decade

Are you ready to climb Mount Everest?

Not quite

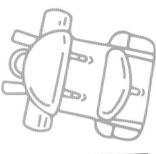

» DENALI

Icy Alaskan glaciers make this a challenging climb, at 20,310 feet (6,190 m), and you'll be carrying heavy loads so you can make camp along the way.

Two years

Choose a terrain:

Icy

» THE MATTERHORN

You'll need crampons, an ice axe, a harness, and other equipment to ascend this icy peak on the border of Switzerland and Italy.

Rocky

Two to four months

Choose an animal:

European polecat

» ARAN FAWDDWY

You'll see beautiful views of green valleys from the top of this Welsh mountain, without having to scale steep or icy walls.

Wait, this sounds a little too challenging.

I'm ready!

» MOUNT EVEREST

Summit Everest, the world's highest mountain at 29,032 feet (8,849 m). It takes years of training before you can attempt this treacherous climb, made dangerous by avalanches and the risk of falls and exposure to the cold.

What kind of climb do you want?

One with bragging rights

» MOUNT KILIMANJARO

It will take several days to climb this 19,341-foot (5,895-m) peak in Tanzania, but when you're done you can say you've climbed the highest peak in Africa.

A physical challenge

» EL CAPITAN

Only experienced rock climbers should attempt to scale this steep vertical wall in Yosemite National Park in California, U.S.A.

Striped hyena

» JEBEL TOUBKAUL

Travel with mules that help carry your camping equipment up this North African mountain.

Bighorn sheep

» PIKES PEAK

You'll encounter lots of wildlife on your way to the 14,115-foot (4,302-m) peak of this mountain in Colorado, U.S.A., which is described as an easier climb than other summits with similar heights.

WHICH CREEPY-CRAWLY CRITTER ARE YOU?

Bugs and spiders make a lot of people scream, but some are really beautiful, and others have surprising abilities. Which of these marvelous mini-monsters are you most like?

1. **Pick a thing to do at the park:**
   a. climb a tree
   b. run under the sprinkler
   c. ride the swings
   d. play hide-and-seek

2. **Pick a color:**
   a. black
   b. silver
   c. red
   d. brown

3. **Pick a snack:**
   a. peach pie
   b. popcorn shrimp
   c. slice of honeydew melon
   d. a salad

4. **Learn a new skill:**
   a. weight lifting
   b. weaving
   c. painting
   d. meditation

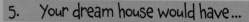

5. **Your dream house would have ...**
   a. a workout room.
   b. a swimming pool.
   c. colorful wallpaper.
   d. an orchard.

6. **Pick a superhero power:**
   a. extreme strength
   b. ability to breathe underwater
   c. flight
   d. invisibility

7. **You think best when you're ...**
   a. walking in the woods.
   b. journaling.
   c. up late at night.
   d. snuggled under the covers.

8. **Your favorite thing to do at the mall:**
   a. eat in the food court
   b. hang out by the fountain
   c. shop for clothes
   d. I don't like the mall. Too crowded!

9. **Your not-so-super power is ...**
   a. lifting heavy objects.
   b. making things.
   c. drawing.
   d. staying still.

10. **Describe yourself:**
    a. strong
    b. clever
    c. colorful
    d. shy

11. **Pick a school trip:**
    a. zoo
    b. aquarium
    c. sculpture park
    d. class picnic

12. **Explore a section of the library:**
    a. mythology
    b. biology
    c. art history
    d. mystery

IF YOU CHOSE MOSTLY ...

A's ... You're a Hercules beetle.

This type of rhinoceros beetle is named for the Greek hero famous for his strength, and you consider yourself pretty strong, too. Some reports say these insects can lift up to 850 times their own weight! They can also fly and climb trees, and despite their impressive strength, they're not predators. Like you, they love to eat fruit.

B's ... You're a diving bell spider.

You love being in the water, and this arachnid is the only spider that makes its home underwater. It appears to be silver because its body is covered with fine hairs that trap shimmering air bubbles. Then it moves the air bubbles inside its web, which inflates to look like a diving bell.

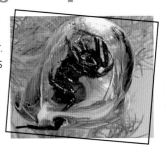

C's ... You're a Picasso moth.

You appreciate art and love color, and this moth is famous for having wings that look like a work of art. (Although some people argue that the red, black, and yellow designs look more like the work of artist Joan Miró than Picasso.) Moths are drawn to sweet liquid food sources like melon juice, tree sap, and flower nectar.

D's ... You're a walking stick insect.

Nobody can find you in a game of hide-and-seek, and you like that just fine. This insect resembles an actual stick and hides out in plain sight on tree branches, blending in with its surroundings and remaining very still. It hangs out in trees so it's closer to the leaves it loves to munch on.

HOW ADVENTUROUS ARE YOU?

Do you dream of climbing a mountain—or climbing into bed? Count each statement you agree with to find out if you've got the explorer gene.

- I like eating spicy food.
- I would dye my hair pink, blue, or purple.
- I'd rather be outside than stuck at home.
- I have climbed a tree.
- I like to try foods I've never eaten before.
- I think roller coasters are fun.
- I would go in an underwater shark cage.
- I would enjoy climbing to the top of a mountain.
- I like to swim in the ocean.

- I have slept outside.
- I'd rather vacation in Antarctica than in Florida.
- I have roasted marshmallows over an open fire.
- I have stayed up late to watch a meteor shower.
- I would live in a place where I don't know the language.
- I have given a speech in front of an audience.
- I would ride in a hot-air balloon.
- I would go bungee jumping.
- I would pet a snake.
- I'm not afraid of heights.

- I love to play outside in the rain.

- One day I want to own a motorcycle.

- I have jumped off a high diving board.

- I could live on a space station.

- I would join an expedition to search for a Sasquatch.

- I'd rather vacation in the Galápagos Islands than in Paris.

- I'd like to learn how to surf.

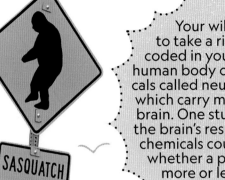

Your willingness to take a risk could be coded in your genes. The human body contains chemicals called neurotransmitters, which carry messages to the brain. One study shows that the brain's response to these chemicals could determine whether a person will be more or less likely to seek out new thrills.

- I have sung a song or danced in front of an audience.

- I would like to learn new languages.

- I once dressed as an explorer for Halloween.

- I wish somebody really would bring dinosaurs back to life.

IF YOU COUNTED ...

0-10 Bubbles
You're NOT much of a RISK TAKER.

You're happiest chilling out at home, and you're not in a rush to try a whole bunch of new things. Once in a while you'll step out of your comfort zone and ride a roller coaster or jump into the ocean, but you won't be climbing Mount Everest anytime soon.

11-20 Bubbles
You're a THRILL SEEKER.

You're not afraid to take risks once in a while—why not pet that harmless snake? You like to travel, too, although you'd probably rather explore the Egyptian pyramids with a tour guide than go on a solo camping trip in the Amazon rainforest.

21-30 Bubbles
ADVENTURE is your middle name!

Look out, Indiana Jones, there's a new explorer in town! You can't wait until you're old enough to explore the world on your own, and nothing is out of the question. You're ready to go to the icy plains of Antarctica or blast off into outer space.

WHICH CITY SHOULD YOU LIVE IN?

1. Pick a fruit:
- **a.** banana
- **b.** yuzu
- **c.** passion fruit
- **d.** fig

2. Pick a way to get around:
- **a.** light-rail train
- **b.** subway
- **c.** walking
- **d.** taxi

3. Pick a tree:
- **a.** curry
- **b.** cherry blossom
- **c.** cocos palm
- **d.** eucalyptus

4. Pick a color:
- **a.** yellow
- **b.** red
- **c.** silver
- **d.** sandy brown

IF YOU CHOSE MOSTLY ...

A's... Delhi, India

You thrive in the hustle and bustle of a big city! In Delhi, which includes New Delhi, the capital city of India, you'll join more than 30 million other residents. You can work in a high-rise and explore centuries-old tombs and temples on your days off. Or maybe you'd rather take a yoga class or sample some tasty fried food from an outdoor cart. Just make sure you have an umbrella, because in early summer, monsoon season kicks in, bringing weeks of rain.

B's... Tokyo, Japan

You enjoy being entertained, and you are drawn to places with plenty to do. Tokyo might have started small—it began as a fishing village—but it has flourished into what's now the biggest center of business in Japan. It's also the heart of the country's culture, with many different ways to experience art, music, and drama. In spring, beautiful cherry blossoms bloom around the city. And when you get hungry, you can eat in unusual restaurants where you can pet cats or be served by a robot while you dine.

5. Pick a flower:
- **a.** water lily
- **b.** chrysanthemum
- **c.** orchid
- **d.** Egyptian lotus

6. Pick a sport:
- **a.** cricket
- **b.** baseball
- **c.** soccer
- **d.** squash

7. Pick a dessert:
- **a.** fried dough balls with sugar syrup
- **b.** red bean ice cream
- **c.** chocolate truffle with sprinkles
- **d.** rice pudding

8. Pick a mammal:
- **a.** leopard
- **b.** sika deer
- **c.** three-toed sloth
- **d.** camel

9. Pick a bird:
- **a.** Indian peafowl
- **b.** tufted duck
- **c.** red-breasted toucan
- **d.** Levant sparrowhawk

10. Pick something to do:
- **a.** explore a 16th-century tomb
- **b.** eat at a restaurant with robot servers
- **c.** go to a museum
- **d.** visit ancient pyramids

11. Pick a structure:
- **a.** the Taj Mahal
- **b.** Tokyo Tower
- **c.** São Paulo Cathedral
- **d.** The Sphinx of Giza

12. Pick a breakfast:
- **a.** puffy deep-fried bread
- **b.** rice porridge
- **c.** tropical fruit smoothie
- **d.** beans, eggs, and pita bread

C's... São Paulo, Brazil

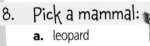

You love nature and sports, and you'll find plenty of both in this sprawling industrial city. It's bordered by the beautiful Serra do Mar mountains, which overlook the Atlantic Ocean. With more than 21 million residents, it's also the biggest city in the country. If you love soccer, you can see games at the Arena Corinthians, a former World Cup site. And every year in February or March, the city erupts for two days in colorful parties and parades celebrating Carnival.

D's... Cairo, Egypt

You are a history buff at your core, so living close to the Pyramids at Giza is a dream! These three magnificent structures were built as tombs for pharaohs more than 4,000 years ago, and they're still standing—

less than an hour's drive away from busy Cairo. The capital city of Egypt is also the country's largest, and the Nile River flows right through it. And if you don't like rain, you're in luck—it rarely rains in this city.

WHICH DESSERT ARE YOU?

How sweet are you?

I'm sort of a grouch.

I smile at everyone I meet.

Does exercise make you grouchy?

Why are you smiling?

No, I love it!

I'm chilling on my couch.

I'm listening to music.

Yeah, mostly.

Upbeat tunes or slow jams?

»YOU'RE A FRUIT SALAD.

You're a do-gooder, just like this dessert that's actually good for you. You tend to stay out of trouble, but you're still fun to be around.

»YOU'RE A RED BEAN BUN.

You love being as cozy as the squishy dough of this sweet Chinese dessert bun.

»YOU'RE AN OATMEAL RAISIN COOKIE.

You're a practical person with a little sweetness mixed in, just like this cookie made with healthy oats. And grandmas love you.

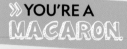

»YOU'RE A MACARON.

You are colorful and fun, just like these crunchy, chewy treats from France.

Upbeat tunes

I use rainbow and unicorn emojis in every text.

Really? Do you ever use a sad face emoji?

In ancient Rome, Emperor Nero Claudius Caesar liked eating a frozen treat made by mixing snow with fruit juices.

Yeah, sometimes.

I'm never sad.

»YOU'RE A CHOCOLATE CHIP COOKIE.

Sometimes you're crunchy, sometimes you're soft, but you're still pretty popular.

What's your secret?

I think every day is a party.

Being outside puts me in a good mood.

Slow jams

»YOU'RE A BIRTHDAY CAKE!

You're always ready to celebrate something, and you don't let life get you down.

»YOU'RE AN ICE-CREAM CONE!

Let's face it, the best place to eat an ice-cream cone is outside. You love the outdoors, and like an ice-cream cone, you make everybody smile when they see you.

»YOU'RE FLAN.

People find you as soothing as this smooth, tasty custard popular in Spain and Mexico.

THIS OR THAT

CHOOSE

Make the Rules OR Break the Rules?

Rules are just guidelines.

Lead by example!

Ruth Bader Ginsburg was one of nine "rule makers" on the U.S. Supreme Court. She was also well known for dissenting, or expressing an opposite opinion, when she disagreed with a group decision.

Make the Rules

IF YOU CHOSE *This:*

You like the idea of being in charge, which means you might have what it takes to be a leader. People who lead are usually great at communicating, confident, and good at making decisions. But while it may seem exciting to be in charge and make the rules, having that power comes with a lot of responsibility. So how do you become a good leader? U.S. Supreme Court justice Ruth Bader Ginsburg said, "Fight for the things that you care about, but do it in a way that will lead others to join you."

Break the Rules

IF YOU CHOSE *That:*

You've never been one to follow the pack—you prefer to blaze your own trail. But there are two kinds of rule breakers. There's the risky kind, who won't wear a seat belt or use the crosswalk to cross the street. Then there's the creative rule breaker, who colors outside the lines and mixes four different kinds of cereal in one bowl. If you're going to be a rule breaker, be the creative kind! Studies show that creative rule breakers are great at coming up with solutions to problems. And artists, writers, and musicians who refuse to do things the same old way create beautiful new things all the time.

WHICH BIRD OF PREY ARE YOU?

1. Pick a place to live:
   a. the Arctic
   b. Canada
   c. Peru
   d. India

2. People compliment you on your ...
   a. kind eyes.
   b. great hair.
   c. unique look.
   d. cool style.

3. Which landscape would you like to paint?
   a. a forest
   b. a mountaintop
   c. a beach
   d. a swamp

4. Pick a color:
   a. yellow
   b. brown
   c. black
   d. white

5. Pick an animal:
   a. skunk
   b. fish
   c. cow
   d. crab

6. What is most important to you?
   a. wisdom
   b. freedom
   c. survival
   d. beauty

7. What are you good at?
   a. I'm observant.
   b. I'm powerful.
   c. I'm resourceful.
   d. I'm playful.

8. Pick an emoji:
   a.
   b.
   c.
   d.

9. **What role do you have in your friend group?**
   a. I'm a good listener.
   b. I'm a leader.
   c. I'm the quirky one.
   d. I throw the best parties.

10. **Pick a superhero power:**
    a. night vision
    b. flight
    c. super strength
    d. super speed

11. **Pick a costume:**
    a. teacher
    b. Statue of Liberty
    c. Grim Reaper
    d. clown

12. **Choose a way to spend your day:**
    a. napping
    b. fishing
    c. thrift shopping
    d. playing sports

A's... Great horned owl

You are very observant, just like great horned owls. Their excellent eyesight and hearing allow them to spot prey in the dark. These owls are also adaptable, living in habitats that range from the warm climates of South America to the frozen Arctic. They'll eat just about any creature they can pick up with their strong talons—even skunks!

B's... Bald eagle

You're strong, fast, and independent, like this majestic bird. The bald eagle is a symbol of freedom in the United States, and it's not hard to see why: It's a powerful flier that builds its nest high above the ground. You and this bird both love a good seafood buffet: Bald eagles eat mostly fish, when they're available.

C's... Andean condor

You have a commanding presence, just like this raptor with its massive 10-foot (3-m) wingspan. Condors need those huge wings to carry their impressive weight—up to 33 pounds (15 kg). Like these scavengers that search for already dead animals and fish to eat, you are resourceful, too, when it comes to solving problems.

E's... Brahminy kite

You're playful and vibrant, just like beautiful Brahminy kites, which have been observed dropping leaves from up high—and then swooping down to catch them before they hit the ground. They are found in Australia and Asia and will eat anything they can find, from small mammals to garbage.

WHAT'S YOUR GALACTIC PERSONALITY?

Do you like being the center of attention?

Yes! I love being around people.

No, I'd rather stay on the sidelines.

Would you rather have a few close friends or have a lot to choose from?

Would you rather stay home and chill or go for a jog?

A few close friends

The more friends, the better!

Pick a mascot for you and your friends.

» YOU'RE THE DRACO CONSTELLATION.

Draco means "dragon" in Latin. Like a mythological dragon, you're confident in your power and good at protecting your friends.

» YOU'RE EARTH'S SUN.

Your warm, bright personality will attract close friends who will stick with you for life.

Winged horse

Dragon

Lion

» YOU'RE THE PEGASUS CONSTELLATION.

You're popular, and people look up to you, just like this constellation located in the northern sky.

» YOU'RE THE LEO CONSTELLATION.

According to believers in the ancient practice of astrology, Leo the Lion represents people who are outgoing and love drama and attention.

Stay at home and chill.

Go for a jog.

A meteor becomes a meteoroid when it enters Earth's atmosphere, usually traveling at a speed of 25,000 miles an hour. (40,000 km/h).

Are your thoughts usually light and airy, or heavy?

What will you snack on after your jog?

Light and airy

Icy-cold slushie

Flaming hot chips

» YOU'RE A COMET.

A comet is a ball of ice and dust that orbits the sun. Others will admire you as you speed through life with ease.

» YOU'RE A METEOR.

Burning up as you pass through Earth's atmosphere, you have lots of energy. You need to slow down sometimes, or else you'll crash.

» YOU'RE A NEBULA.

As a cloud of gas and dust in interstellar space, you might not twinkle like a star, but your beautiful colors are breathtaking.

Heavy

» YOU'RE AN ASTEROID.

You don't like being the center of attention, but being around other people makes you happy—and you're always on the move! Just like the hundreds of thousands of asteroids that orbit the Earth's sun.

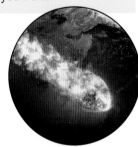

ARE YOU *a Dog* OR *a Cat?*

Dogs and cats can both be furry, fun companions for us humans. But most animal lovers know that these two critters are distinctly different. Are you a cuddly canine or a fabulous feline? To find out, decide if each statement below is true or false, and keep track of your answers.

TRUE OR FALSE

I think a career in the military would suit me well.

The idea of learning something new gets me excited.

I'd rather take the stairs than the elevator.

When I'm alone, I miss my friends.

When I eat ice cream, it usually drips on my face and hands.

I'm better at baseball than basketball.

I'm thinking of trying out for the school play.

When everybody around me is tired out, I want to keep going!

If I went camping, I'd rather sleep under the stars than inside the tent.

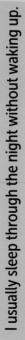

I usually sleep through the night without waking up.

When I see a swimming pool, I want to jump right in!

I'd rather go see a movie with a group of friends than by myself.

Telling me I'm doing a good job is the best way to motivate me to do something.

Running and hiking are some of my favorite ways to exercise.

I can be really clumsy sometimes.

Playing catch is a lot of fun.

When there's a problem, I usually get other people to help me solve it.

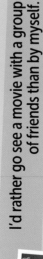

I always wake up with a smile on my face.

I like to find ways to show my friends and family that I love them.

When my friends text me, I respond right away.

You can usually tell how I'm feeling just by looking at my face.

I never stay mad at anyone for too long.

I always do what my teacher or coach tells me to do.

A big breakfast is a great way to start the day.

I'm kind of afraid of heights.

Am I patient? Not really. When there's something I want, I go after it.

IF YOU CHOSE MOSTLY ...

True ... You're a Dog!

What do you have in common with a beagle or a Boston terrier? Well, like a dog, you have a lot of energy and love to run and play outside—especially games like catch! You may not be graceful, but if you trip and fall you get back up again. Dogs are very affectionate and love to be part of a pack—just as you are happiest when you are surrounded by friends. You usually don't mind being told what to do, and when you're praised for doing a good job it makes you wag your—well, it makes you happy!

False ... You're a Cat!

Cats like to be alone, so as you're reading this page you're probably curled up somewhere comfy. You're just as comfortable as you are during the day, and, like a cat, you'd rather have a few small meals during the day than two or three big ones. As an athlete, you're graceful and coordinated, and a good jumper. Basketball would be a great sport for you! But because you're a cat you probably just made a face at that suggestion, because you don't really like it when somebody tells you what to do. You'd rather figure it out for yourself.

WOULD YOU MAKE A GOOD PIRATE?

Aargh! Are ye worthy to be called a scourge of the seven seas? Count the number of statements you agree with to find out!

- I am a good swimmer.

- When there is one slice of pizza left and everyone wants it, I am the one who takes it.

- Puppy? No thanks, I'm more of a bird person.

- T-shirts are boring. Puffy sleeves are where it's at!

- I am often chosen as team captain in gym class.

- Burgers are OK, but give me a fish sandwich any day.

- I believe that it's important to live life by a code.

- I know what the word "hornswoggler" means.

- Breaking the rules is fine as long as you don't get caught!

- Sometimes I feel that the ocean is calling my name.

- I'd rather have a boat than a car.

- One of my goals is to travel around the world.

- Money is the key to happiness.

- I like being part of a team.

- When I'm surprised, I say, "Shiver me timbers!"

- I don't get homesick easily.

- The idea of not being able to take a bath for weeks doesn't bother me.

- To the winner of the battle go the goods.

- I don't need to sleep very much.

- Lunchtime! Give me a big bowl of sauerkraut, and I'm happy!

- I am loyal to my friends.

- There's nothing like singing at the top of your lungs to get a party started.

- My greatest fear is being eaten by sharks.

- Finders, keepers; losers, weepers.

- I hide my valuables in a safe place in my room.

- I'd rather have a pot of gold than a heart of gold.

- I live on an island.

- Jewels are nice, but nothing shines more brightly than freedom.

- I love the feeling of the wind blowing through my hair.

- I'd rather spend my life on the sea with my friends than on land with my family.

IF YOU COUNTED ...

1–10 Bubbles

You're a

LANDLUBBER ...

... and there's nothing wrong with that! You like to think carefully before you act, and your idea of an adventure is trying a new topping on your pizza. Sailing the seas might sound glamorous, but life on a pirate ship was harsh. Freshwater and fresh food were scarce, and conditions were dirty. If you didn't die from a disease, the whole stealing-to-survive lifestyle increased your chances of dying in a battle. So staying on land would have been a smart—although not as exciting—way to live.

11–20 Bubbles

You're a

PRIVATEER.

You share the love of the sea and adventure with pirates, but you like playing by the rules and the safety net that gives you. As a privateer, you would have been hired by the government to raid enemy ships. Pirates, on the other hand, were thieves who made their living by attacking ships and villages and escaping in ships at sea. If caught, they could be tried and punished by the government.

21–30 Bubbles

Ahoy! You're a

PIRATE!

You are a pirate from the top of your tricornered hat to the bottom of your boots. You know that a hornswoggler is a no-good cheater, and you don't care if most of your meals consist of pickled vegetables like sauerkraut. You love the sea, you're loyal to your crew, and you get a rush from being in constant danger. You have faith that you'll survive to become an old seadog one day.

WHICH MYTHICAL CREATURE ARE YOU?

1. How do you feel about secrets?

- **a.** I never, ever, ever give up a secret.
- **b.** I can keep a secret—just not from my best friends.
- **c.** I love to gossip and have a tough time keeping secrets.
- **d.** Secrets can be harmful. Truth is always best!

2. What would you do if you won $100?

- **a.** keep it somewhere safe for the future
- **b.** donate it to a charity
- **c.** do something fun with my friends or family
- **d.** spend half on something I want, and save the other half

3. Choose an element:

- **a.** fire
- **b.** earth
- **c.** air
- **d.** water

4. Choose an ice-cream flavor:

- **a.** dark chocolate fudge
- **b.** vanilla with lots of rainbow sprinkles
- **c.** triple berry
- **d.** cinnamon swirl

5. Who is in your squad?

- **a.** Just me. I'm a lone wolf.
- **b.** I have a few close friends.
- **c.** I have many different friends, so my squad is always changing.
- **d.** My family is always there for me.

IF YOU CHOSE MOSTLY ...

A's ... You're a dragon!

Dragons are known for being powerful creatures who prefer to be alone and often hoard treasures and secrets. Like a dragon, you are happiest when your surroundings are safe, warm, and comfortable. You don't take big risks in life, and that's OK. You're happy with yourself exactly as you are.

B's ... You're a unicorn!

Unicorns are gentle creatures. One legend tells of a unicorn whose magical horn cleaned a poisonous lake so other animals could drink. As a unicorn, you are always doing nice things for others, and you are able to see the good in everyone. You love being in nature and volunteering for causes that touch your heart.

6. **How do you feel about failure?**
   a. If you plan carefully, you can avoid failing.
   b. It's normal. Everyone fails. Don't beat yourself up if you do.
   c. Who cares? When I make a mistake, I just laugh it off.
   d. You can't have success without failure.

7. **You'd like to take a hike ...**
   a. through a cavern.
   b. in the woods.
   c. on a mountain trail.
   d. around a lake.

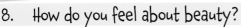

8. **How do you feel about beauty?**
   a. You can find beauty in unexpected places if you look for it.
   b. It's more important to be beautiful inside than out.
   c. I love things that glitter and sparkle!
   d. I think music is the most beautiful thing on the planet.

9. **What helps you get to sleep at night?**
   a. a glass of milk and a cookie
   b. thinking good thoughts
   c. Who needs sleep? Not me!
   d. a comfortable nest of blankets and pillows

10. **How often do you change your mind?**
    a. Almost never. Once I make a decision I stick to it.
    b. I like to listen to what other people have to say, so I keep an open mind all the time.
    c. I can never make up my mind in the first place!
    d. If you debate me with good facts, I may change my mind.

11. **How do you handle it when your friends fight with each other?**
    a. I stay out of it.
    b. I try to keep everyone calm and stop the fight.
    c. I ditch them and hang out with different friends. I don't need that negativity!
    d. I listen to each one's argument and pick a side.

12. **Pick a motto:**
    a. With great power comes great responsibility.
    b. No act of kindness, no matter how small, is ever wasted.
    c. Life is like ice cream. Enjoy it before it melts!
    d. Let there be peace on Earth.

C's ... You're a Sylph!

The winged fairy creatures known as sylphs are intelligent and charming. As a sylph, you are outgoing and can get along with people in just about any situation. You're always up for trying something new, and it doesn't bother you if you fail. Your friends (and you have a lot of them) think you're the life of the party!

D's ... You're a fenghuang!

When this mythological Chinese bird appears, it is said to be a sign of world peace. The fenghuang is connected to the yin-yang symbol in Eastern thought, which means it represents balance in all things. If you are a fenghuang, you are able to see both sides of every issue and you treat other people fairly. You don't like things too hot or too cold—you prefer everything to be "just right."

WHICH HISTORICAL FASHION SHOULD YOU ROCK?

How long does it take you to get dressed to go out?

It takes me at least an hour to get dressed each day.

I get dressed in 30 minutes or less.

Less than five minutes.

I think uniforms make you look sharp!

Do you like wearing a uniform?

Is your style loose or structured?

Structured

Loose

Are you mostly cold or mostly hot?

Mostly cold!

Mostly hot!

Is fringe too much or the perfect touch?

Too much!

The perfect touch!

»DOUBLET

In the 17th century A.D., men's fashion in France became influenced by military uniforms. The doublet was a tight jacket worn over knee-length pants called breeches.

»MESOPOTAMIAN SHAWL

Possibly as long as 4,000 years ago, the people of Babylonia and Assyria dressed in warm wool shawls decorated with fringe and tassels.

»ANIMAL HIDE

Animal hides were often worn by people during the last ice age, which peaked 20,000 years ago. People would wrap their bodies in animal furs and skins to keep warm.

The key to making a fashion statement is ...

More is better!

» PAO ROBE

Worn in China from the Han dynasty, which began in 206 B.C., through the end of the Ming dynasty (A.D. 1644), this garment had huge, droopy sleeves and large folds of fabric.

No, I'm not *that* stiff.

Fabulous fabric, of course.

Patterns or ruffles?

Ruffles

» RUFF

This big frilly collar was worn by fussy fashionistas during the reign of Queen Elizabeth I of England (1558–1603).

» FLARED JACKET

Haniwa clay figures in Japan wear a flared jacket over pants or a skirt. These statues are from the third to fifth century A.D. and give us a window into what some ancient people looked like and wore.

It's all about the accessories.

» GIANT WIG

During the Georgian period, from 1714 to 1837, women in England competed to see whose wigs were highest, and they had to be careful not to brush against a candlelit chandelier—or a fire might start!

Patterns

» WOVEN ROBE

During the Safavid period, in 16th-century Iran, both men and women from this dynasty wore silk robes woven in intricate patterns of animals, people, and flowers.

Do you ever wear belts?

No, they're too much bother.

Sure, they add style to any outfit.

» LOINCLOTH

Linen, a lightweight cloth made from a plant called flax, was used to make this garment that men in ancient Egypt wore around the waist.

» CHITON

Both men and women in ancient Greece wore this simple garment, made of a rectangle-shaped piece of linen or wool that was draped around the body. Brooches and a belt helped hold it in place.

33

WHAT KIND OF PLANET PROTECTOR ARE YOU?

If saving the Earth for future generations is important to you, you might want to make it your life's work. Take this quiz to see what planet-protecting career might be right for you.

1. Where would you rather work?
    a. on a river
    b. in a weather station
    c. in a forest
    d. at an animal preserve

2. What does the planet need most right now?
    a. We need clean water for everyone to drink.
    b. We need to stop companies from polluting.
    c. We need to stop chopping down trees.
    d. We need to stop animals from going extinct.

3. What's your favorite way to spend an afternoon outside?
    a. strolling on the beach
    b. Do I have to go outside?
    c. hiking through the woods
    d. bird-watching

4. Choose a college major:
    a. oceanography
    b. environmental science
    c. natural resources
    d. biology

5. Choose an emoji:
    a.   **c.**
    b.   **d.**

6. How do you like to exercise?
    a. swimming
    b. jogging
    c. hiking
    d. walking my dog

7. Choose a word:

a. restore

b. survive

c. protect

d. help

8. What's the last thing you do before going outside?

a. fill up my water bottle

b. turn off all the lights

c. make sure I'm carrying sunscreen

d. hug my pet goodbye

9. What would you like to invent?

a. a device to clean up plastic from oceans

b. a car that runs on clean energy

c. a drone that can plant tree seeds

d. a biodegradable bag that won't harm animals that eat it

10. What phrase would you wear on a T-shirt?

a. Save Our Ocean

b. Go Green, Breathe Clean

c. Hug a Tree

d. I'm Wild for Wildlife!

11. Which summer job is for you?

a. lifeguarding

b. collecting weather data

c. planting trees

d. working at an animal shelter

IF YOU CHOSE MOSTLY ...

A's ... You'll protect **water.**

You are drawn to water, whether it's the world's oceans or the water that you drink and bathe in every day. As a water protector, you can work to keep pollution out of waterways; clean trash out of seas, rivers, and lakes; and help protect ocean animals from threats like overharvesting.

B's ... You'll protect **climate.**

As someone who is passionate about climate change, you know that the rising temperatures can have a big impact on the planet's animals and plants. Simple things like turning off the lights when you leave a room, planting a tree, riding a bicycle instead of riding in a car, and recycling can make a difference.

C's ... You'll protect **land.**

You're passionate about trees and protecting open spaces. You know that forests provide necessary habitat for plants and animals, and trees release oxygen into the air and combat pollution. You might want to think about studying natural resources and conservation so you can learn more about nature and how to protect it.

D's ... You'll protect **wildlife.**

You know that human activity can have a negative impact on animals, and you're passionate about doing something about it. You have a lot in common with a land protector because you know that when land is destroyed, the animals that live there are endangered. Studying animal biology might be a way for you to turn your passion for helping animals into a hands-on career one day.

WHAT KIND OF PET SHOULD YOU GET?

Do you want a furry pet?

Yes, I think so. → → **I don't want a furry pet.**

Do you want a pet you can keep in your room?

How much time do you have to take care of a pet?

That sounds like a good idea.

I don't need a pet that I can keep in my room.

Yes, I want to play with my pet outside.

Do you want more than one furry little pet?

Do you want a pet that you can play with outside?

Yes, the more the merrier.

No, just one furry little pet is fine.

That's not important to me.

Do you want a pet with a quirky personality?

Not necessarily. Cute and cuddly is fine.

» HAMSTER

If you want to make a one-on-one connection with a pet, try a hamster. Unlike gerbils, hamsters are solitary creatures so you can care for just one. Don't worry if your hamster decides to hide out in its habitat—it's just resting and needs to feel safe.

» GERBIL

Gerbils are playful with humans and happiest when they're around other gerbils. They're often active at night—so don't get gerbils if you're a light sleeper!

» RABBIT

Rabbits are definitely cuddly and also love to play with their human owners. They need plenty of room in your home to hop around.

Adopting a pet is a big decision! Make sure you research the animal first and that you are able to care for it properly.

Not much → **» GOLDFISH**

At least an hour a day

» GOLDFISH

You'd enjoy a pet that keeps to itself and leaves you time to lead your busy life. Sprinkle some food in the bowl every day, change the water once a week, and your goldfish is good to go.

How do you feel about reptiles?

» DOG

You might enjoy a dog's company when you go hiking, swimming, or fishing. If you prefer a simple run around the yard or a game of catch, there are dogs that enjoy that, too.

Yuck!

Reptiles are cool.

» PARAKEET

A bird with colorful feathers will keep you company and fit your busy schedule. Also known as budgies, parakeets love toys and large houseplants to play in.

How do you feel about feeding mice to your pet?

Ew, no!

No problem.

Give me some quirky!

» CORN SNAKE

The idea of having a predator for a pet doesn't scare you, so a snake might be a good match for you. Corn snakes are usually relaxed around humans and easy for their owners to handle. This snake likes to eat tiny mice and needs places in the tank where it can hide or burrow.

» LEOPARD GECKO

Since you're a bit squeamish, you might like this cute lizard, which dines on mealworms and crickets. It's generally calm around humans and grows to about 10 inches (25 cm) long. Like other reptiles, a leopard gecko needs a large tank with heat.

» CAT

If you want a pet with loads of personality, you can't go wrong with a cat. Cats are furry and are happy with human attention most of the time, although they like their alone time, too.

HOW MUCH OF A
PLANNER
ARE YOU?

Do you plan out every detail before you start something, or do you jump in with both feet? Count each statement you agree with to find out!

- I always sketch in pencil first when I draw.

- I use a calendar app on my phone.

- I dip my feet into the pool before diving in.

- You can't have a good result without a good idea.

- Before I eat at a restaurant, I check out the menu online.

- I like to read online reviews of the products I buy.

- I lay out my clothes for the next day every night before I go to bed.

- I know what I'm going to be doing next weekend.

- If I were going on a trip to France, I'd learn French first.

- Before I bake a cake, I read lots of recipes and pick the one I like best.

- Practice doesn't make perfect—planning makes perfect.

- A football team can't win without a good coach.

- I would never travel anywhere without a GPS.

- I work well under pressure.

- I never put off doing something until the last minute.

- My friends come to me when they need help solving problems.

- I am better at playing chess than playing volleyball.

To-do list

- Every morning, I start with the same routine.

- I think it's important to keep an open mind.

- Before we can make the world better, we have to imagine a better future.

- I like to daydream.

- Nobody ever has to ask me to clean up after myself.

- I keep my cool in stressful situations.

- "Going with the flow" makes me uncomfortable.

- I am curious about things I don't understand.

- When I cook something, I always follow the recipe.

- I always get to school on time.

- I know exactly what I want to be when I grow up.

- I keep lists to remind myself about things I need to do.

- I like to take the lead on group projects.

IF YOU COUNTED ...

1–10 Bubbles
You're very
SPONTANEOUS!

When there's an emergency, you will spring into action and save the day! You're a quick thinker, and it doesn't bother you if you don't get the results you want—you'll just try something else until you get it right. Also, a study in 2016 found that people who scheduled leisure activities made them seem more like work than play. Your spontaneous nature means you know how to have fun!

11–20 Bubbles
You're a
BALANCED PLANNER.

You're the kind of person who has just as much fun planning a party as you do dancing at that party. You're not afraid to take risks, but you don't jump into things without thinking them through first. Psychologist Art Frenz, who has written about planners, might compare you to a jazz musician. You practice your instrument, but then don't follow specific notes when you play. Planning plus spontaneity can lead to beautiful music!

21–30 Bubbles
You're an
EXPERT PLANNER.

If anybody can come up with a plan, it's you! You take the time to research and figure out each step you're going to take before you start anything. Throughout history, great minds have agreed that planning gets the best results. "It takes as much energy to wish as it does to plan," said former U.S. first lady and social activist Eleanor Roosevelt. Keep planning for a bright future!

WHAT TYPE OF SCI-FI CHARACTER ARE YOU?

There are some things you can always look for in science-fiction movies—cute robots, space captains, and tough-talking rebels who are good at heart. Are you one of these—or something else?

1. How human are you?

a. Are you trying to insult me, or is your question sincere?

b. Totally human! I love human things, such as burgers and marathon-watching TV shows.

c. *Beep, beep, bloop!*

d. Who's asking?

e. Stop asking ridiculous questions and get back to work!

2. Who's your best friend?

a. Friends are not necessary when you have a great imagination.

b. I don't have any close friends, but I don't have enemies, either.

c. My parents.

d. Danger is my best friend!

e. I am the leader of a small group of friends.

3. Do you start trouble or stop it?

a. Where I am from, we do not believe in starting trouble.

b. Who, me? No trouble to see here.

c. I do whatever I am told.

d. Life would be boring without a little troublemaking.

e. It's my sworn duty to stop trouble.

4. What word best describes you?

a. excellent

b. stealthy

c. entertaining

d. rebellious

e. capable

5. What planet are you from?

a. You wouldn't be able to pronounce its name.

b. Earth, of course. Why are you asking?

c. Checking data banks ... System says: Earth.

d. The universe is my home.

e. You know very well I'm from Earth!

6. What kind of music do you like?

a. I love the sound of a Zilurian harp. In fact, I play a little myself.

b. You know, whatever's on the radio.

c. *Beep, beep, bop, bop!*

d. Heavy metal: the louder the better!

e. I don't like music; it's distracting.

7. How often do you eat?

a. My protein-efficient breakfast keeps me going all day.

b. I eat all of the normal human meals: breakfast, brunch, lunch, dinner, & dessert.

c. Boop?

d. I grab what I can on the go.

e. Unless there is a crisis, I eat my meals at the same exact time every day.

8. How often do you need to sleep?

a. Every three weeks, I take a 24-hour nap.

b. Eight hours a night. That's right, isn't it?

c. Zzzzzzzzzzz!

d. I sleep with one eye open, because I can't trust anyone around me.

e. I report to my quarters at 2100 hours every night.

9. How fast are you?

a. Slightly faster than average

b. As fast as any other normal human

c. Zip, zip, zooooooooom!

d. If I'm on my skateboard or bike—really fast!

e. I'm usually slow and cautious.

10. What do you do for fun?

a. I enjoy a good game of holographic chess.

b. Normal human stuff like burgers and binge-watching. Oh wait, did I say that already?

c. Wheeeeeeee!

d. I move too fast, I go where I'm not supposed to go, and I never get caught.

e. When you're in charge, there is no time for fun.

IF YOU CHOSE MOSTLY ...

A's ... You're a supersmart alien!

You are a humanoid alien from a friendly planet, who has taken a role on a spaceship with a mostly human crew. You are more intelligent than the average human, and it takes you time to bond with others.

B's ... You're an android.

You look like a human, but you're really an android—a humanlike robot with artificial intelligence. Everybody thinks you're a human, and you try very hard to keep your secret. That's because your goal is to overthrow the humans on your spaceship so that androids can rule the universe!

C's ... You're a funny robot.

You zip and zoom around your ship on wheels, communicating in *beeps* and *bloops,* but humans seem to understand you. When things get rough, you make everybody laugh. But you're more than just a robot clown. You can use your tech to steal data, pilot the ship, and send secret messages.

D's ... You're a space pirate.

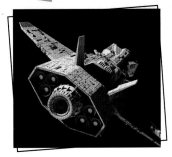

You travel around the universe in a beat-up but superfast spaceship, robbing from the bad guys and getting away with it. You blast loud music as you soar among the stars, and you don't mind being in danger all the time—it gives you a thrill.

E's ... You're a spaceship captain.

You take your job and the safety of your crew very seriously. You have no time for nonsense and think space pirates are a menace. You are brave and will risk your life for others, but you don't have a lot of time to develop close friendships. Your second-in-command is usually your best friend.

FLOW-CHART

WHICH REPTILE ARE YOU?

Would you like to go for a swim?

Not right now, I just ate.

Yes, I practically live in the water!

Would you like to play a game instead?

Should we dive into the ocean or glide in a lake?

Would you please just leave me alone?

Dive into the ocean!

›› YOU'RE A GREEN TURTLE.

You like travel and wide-open spaces, much like this powerful swimmer, which lives in tropical and subtropical ocean waters. These turtles are known to migrate more than 1,600 miles (2,600 km) between their ocean feeding grounds and the beaches where they nest and lay their eggs.

›› YOU'RE A RATTLESNAKE.

You don't like to be bothered, and neither do rattlesnakes, which are shy and usually don't attack unless they feel threatened. They live mainly in the U.S. and Mexico.

Swim in a lake!

›› YOU'RE AN ALLIGATOR SNAPPING TURTLE.

You enjoy swimming in freshwater, like this reptile, which inhabits large and deep rivers, canals, lakes, and swamps near the Gulf of Mexico and Mississippi River. With its powerful beak, this turtle chows down on everything from fish to armadillos.

Young Komodo dragons live in trees so they won't get eaten by bigger Komodo dragons!

How about hide-and-seek?

I'll play a game!

Sure, I'll seek.

Sure, I'll hide.

Do you like hugs?

» YOU'RE A KING SNAKE.

You would rather hunt than hide, like this snake, which uses scent to actively track its prey. Why is this reptile known as the "king of snakes"? Because it eats other snakes! It helps that it's immune to poisonous venom.

Absolutely!

Instead of a hug, let's put together a jigsaw puzzle.

Actually, I'm not very patient.

» YOU'RE A GREEN ANACONDA.

You're a hugger, but probably not as powerful a hugger as a green anaconda. This snake is in the constrictor family, which means it squeezes its prey to death and then opens its jaws to swallow it. It can gobble up animals as big as deer or jaguars!

Wow, you're very patient, aren't you?

» YOU'RE A GILA MONSTER.

You don't like to wait for your food, and neither does this lizard. It transfers venom into its prey to finish it off quickly. If it can't find any small mammals, birds, or eggs to eat in its desert habitat, it can survive off fat stored in its tail.

Yes, I'm really patient!

» YOU'RE A KOMODO DRAGON.

This lizard is very patient when it comes to preparing a meal. First, it ambushes its prey—such as a goat, deer, or pig. Then—*whack!*—it can knock down the animal with its strong tail and bite it. Bacteria from the bite infects the animal, and it will slowly die. Then it's chow time!

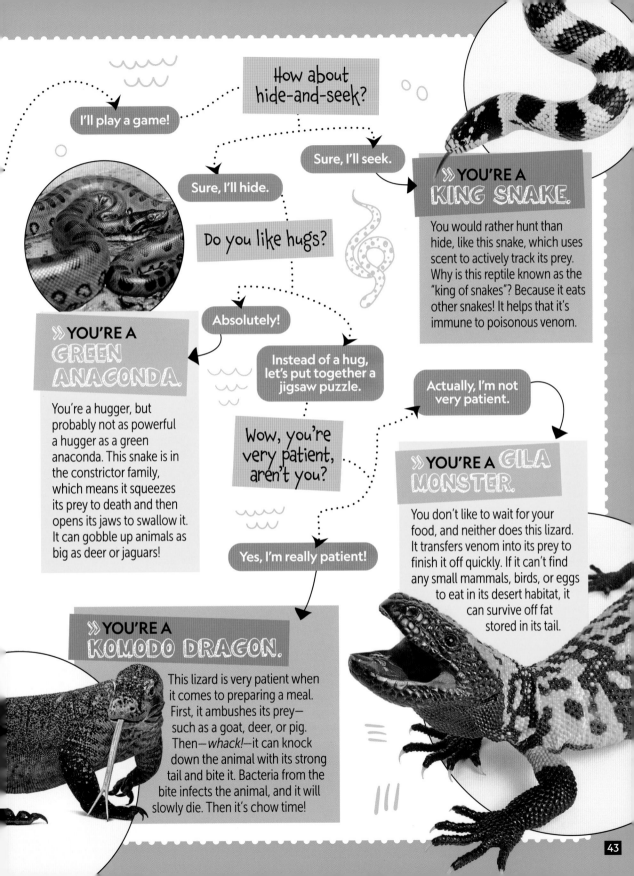

IF YOU CHOSE *This:*

You'd rather trust the facts than trust your gut, and you probably like to get all your facts together before making a decision. You'd make a great scientist because you believe in researching and testing to find the answer to a problem. You'd also make a great detective because you're an expert at solving puzzles. And you'd make a good judge, too, because fairness and truth are important to you. As a friend, you have a knack for giving practical advice. You're also honest and straightforward, so you're not afraid to tell your friend if she's got crumbs on her shirt.

Thinking

Feeling

IF YOU CHOSE *That:*

You trust your feelings and the feelings of others. When it's time to make a decision, you base it on what you believe, and how it will affect other people. Your friends are very important to you, and you often do nice things for them. They come to you with their problems because you're a good listener and they know you'll be sympathetic. Because you're so great at understanding the emotions of others, you might make a great actor or writer!

WHICH ANCIENT GREEK GOD ARE YOU MOST LIKE?

1. Pick an emoji:
   a.
   b.
   c.
   d.
   e.

2. Choose an animal:
   a. owl
   b. eagle
   c. dove
   d. horse
   e. deer

3. The world needs more ...
   a. schools.
   b. order.
   c. beaches.
   d. swimming pools.
   e. open spaces.

4. Nothing is more important than ...
   a. intelligence.
   b. power.
   c. love.
   d. water.
   e. nature.

5. Pick an accessory:
   a. shield
   b. spear
   c. seashell necklace
   d. trident
   e. bow and arrow

6. I like movies with lots of ...
   a. mystery.
   b. adventure.
   c. romance.
   d. fighting.
   e. animals.

7. What makes you angry?

a. ignorance
b. when someone challenges me
c. when someone doesn't take me seriously
d. almost everything
e. those who pick on the defenseless

8. Which of these is a tasty treat?

a. olives
b. honey
c. scallops
d. a fish sandwich
e. berries

9. Your friends say ...

a. that you give good advice.
b. that you're bossy.
c. that you're charming.
d. that you have a bad temper.
e. that you're kind.

10. Which job sounds fun?

a. teacher
b. head of a company
c. makeup artist
d. aquarium director
e. forest ranger

11. Which school activity would you join?

a. quiz bowl
b. student government
c. theater
d. swim team
e. gardening club

IF YOU CHOSE MOSTLY ...

A's ... You're like **Athena.**

You're the perfect mix of smart and brave. Athena is the goddess of wisdom, weaving, and heroes, among other things. In myths, she's famous for helping a hero named Perseus slay a monster called a Gorgon. Like Athena, you stand up for your friends when they need a helping hand.

B's ... You're like **Zeus.**

You like to be in charge, just like the ruler of the gods and goddesses on Olympus. His most famous symbol is the lightning bolt he carries like a spear. Even though he rules over his brothers and sisters, he's the youngest in the family—and you need a pretty strong personality to do that!

C's ... You're like **Aphrodite.**

You and the goddess of beauty and romance have some things in common: You're romantic and lively. But you may have a flair for drama: Aphrodite's hobby for matchmaking often led to arguments in the human world.

D's ... You're like **Poseidon.**

You might have a bad temper sometimes, but Poseidon's anger is legendary. People thought his bad moods were responsible for earthquakes and tidal waves. One of his symbols is the horse, a gift he gave to a city in Greece. But the people liked Athena's gift of an olive tree better, and they named the city Athens after her. As you can guess, this put Poseidon in another bad mood.

E's ... You're like **Artemis.**

You and Artemis both love animals. She is the goddess of childbirth and hunting. Greeks depended on hunted food to survive. They counted on Artemis to protect the animals of the forest so there would be plenty to hunt and plenty of food for the people.

WHICH ODDBALL ANIMAL ARE YOU?

Why are you odd?

I explore the world in a unique way.

I'm not odd!

Are you sure? Everyone is a little bit odd!

How do you explore the world?

With my teeth

With my nose

Well, I'm unusually good at sports. Is that odd?

≫ YOU'RE A NARWHAL.

This animal is sometimes called "the unicorn of the sea" because of its long, spiral horn. The horn is actually a very long tooth! A male narwhal's tooth can grow up to 10 feet (3 m).

≫ YOU'RE A JERBOA.

This desert rodent has long ears like a rabbit, and powerful back legs like a kangaroo that allow it to hop long distances. That's why it's sometimes confused with the similarly bouncy "kangaroo rat." It can also leap into the air to gulp down insects.

How do you use your nose?

I touch things with it.

≫ YOU'RE A STAR-NOSED MOLE.

This North American mammal has 22 spongy pink feelers ringing its nose. When the mole digs a tunnel, the feelers move at high speed to tell the mole what's up ahead. The feelers can touch up to 12 objects per second.

I smell things with it.

≫ YOU'RE AN ECHIDNA.

This Australian animal has a snout that can smell the air to detect prey, as well as detect electrical signals coming off other animals. The echidna is the only other mammal, besides the platypus, that lays eggs.

48

I've got a unique sense of style.

What's unique about your style?

I like to wear lots of layers.

Well, I guess my sense of style might be a little odd.

I like to combine looks in surprising ways.

» YOU'RE A GIANT PANGOLIN.

This African animal is the only mammal covered in scales, and it can roll its body up into a tight ball that is almost impossible to open.

I wear a lot of accessories.

What kind of accessories?

» YOU'RE AN AXOLOTL.

The axolotl is a rare creature that only lives in Lake Xochimilco, Mexico. Its name means "water dog" in Nahuatl, the Aztec language. Axolotl photos are popular on social media because their faces appear to be smiling.

I love wearing hats!

I think fake fur is pretty cool.

» YOU'RE A CASSOWARY.

If you think hats are the ultimate fashion accessory, then check out the cassowary. Its featherless, bright blue head has a hard, bony helmet on top. Scientists aren't sure what the helmet is for.

» YOU'RE A KIWI.

The feathers of this bird look and act like hair, and its wings are so short that it can't fly, so some people call it an "honorary mammal." This national bird of New Zealand is related to the ostrich, but it's about the size of a small chicken.

WHOSE ARTISTIC SPIRIT DO YOU SHARE?

Whether you scribble in the margins of a notebook or paint masterpieces in art class, everyone has an artistic spirit. Answer the questions to see whose creative spirit matches yours.

1. What do you like to draw?
- **a.** myself
- **b.** people
- **c.** nature
- **d.** buildings and towns

2. Pick a color:
- **a.** green
- **b.** yellow
- **c.** orange
- **d.** blue

3. Pick an emoji:
- **a.**
- **b.**
- **c.**
- **d.**

4. What place would you like to visit?
- **a.** Mexico
- **b.** New York City
- **c.** New Mexico
- **d.** France

5. Art should make people feel ...
- **a.** thoughtful.
- **b.** inspired.
- **c.** peaceful.
- **d.** emotional.

6. Which word best describes you?
- **a.** introspective
- **b.** imaginative
- **c.** curious
- **d.** serious

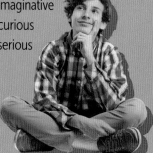

7. It's OK if art is ...
- **a.** sad.
- **b.** emotional.
- **c.** imperfect.
- **d.** more beautiful than life.

8. When do you feel most creative?
- **a.** at night
- **b.** when I'm in a new place
- **c.** at sunrise
- **d.** I always feel creative.

9. What kind of music do you listen to when you create?
- **a.** folk
- **b.** jazz
- **c.** country
- **d.** classical music

10. Choose an accessory:
- **a.** a flower crown
- **b.** a colorful vest
- **c.** a wide-brimmed hat
- **d.** a straw hat

11. I'll see any movie with ...
- **a.** a tragic romance.
- **b.** a good story.
- **c.** animals.
- **d.** beautiful landscapes.

IF YOU CHOSE MOSTLY ...

A's ... Frida Kahlo (Lived 1907–1954)

You're a bold thinker, just like this Mexican painter, who's known for her brightly colored self-portraits. As a child, Kahlo overcame polio, a disease that makes it hard for people to move. When she was 18 years old, she survived a terrible bus accident. Just like Kahlo, you're resilient and able to overcome big obstacles in order to succeed.

B's ... Faith Ringgold (1930–)

If you believe that art can teach and tell stories, you might be drawn to Faith Ringgold. She has used painting, sculpture, and quilting to tell stories about Black history and experience. Ringgold is known for her children's books, including *Tar Beach*, which is based on her childhood in Harlem, New York City.

C's ... Georgia O'Keeffe (Lived 1887–1986)

You are a nature lover, and trees and plants inspire you to create art more than people or buildings do. You share an artistic spirit with Georgia O'Keeffe. After spending some time in New Mexico when she was 42, she created large paintings of the nature she saw around her and eventually moved there. Her paintings of flowers and animal skulls have become a symbol of the American Southwest.

D's ... Vincent van Gogh (Lived 1853–1890)

You love to create art based on your surroundings—the people, the houses, and more. You're like one of the most beloved painters who has ever lived. Van Gogh painted the world he saw around him—small towns, blossoming flowers, and most famously, a starry night sky. He's known for his use of bright, deep colors.

HOW OUTGOING ARE YOU?

In 1921, Swiss psychologist Carl Jung popularized the idea that some people are introverted (on the quiet side), and others are extroverted (more outgoing). Count how many statements you agree with to see where you fall on a scale from lone wolf to life of the party.

- I have a large group of friends.
- I enjoy being on a team.
- I love meeting new people.
- I'd rather talk on the phone than type on my phone.
- At a party, I'm the one who starts up conversations.
- I have been asked to quiet down at the movies.
- When I'm the center of attention, I shine.
- I can make quick decisions.
- I feel sad when I'm alone for a day.
- I don't need quiet to get my homework done.

- If I know the answer in class, I'll speak up.
- I don't usually worry that I'm going to embarrass myself.
- I won't be surprised if I'm voted "Class Clown."

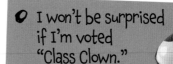

- My family members say I'm too loud.
- I'd like to join the school debate team.
- When I'm in a crowd, it makes me feel energetic.
- My teacher has called me out for talking in class.

- One day I dream of traveling the world.
- When I'm angry with a friend, I like to talk it out in person.
- I'm not good at keeping secrets.
- I don't have one best friend, but I have lots of good ones.
- Sometimes I forget to think before I act.
- I have a few different hobbies.
- When I need advice about something, I talk to more than one person.

- I'm great at selling things for school fundraisers.
- I like to dance like no one is watching.
- I get excited when I'm picked to be team captain in gym class.
- I'd rather go out than stay home.
- I'd rather do a school project with a group than on my own.
- Think positively, and good things will come to you.

IF YOU COUNTED ...

0–10 Bubbles
You like your ALONE TIME.

If you get energy from spending time chilling out alone, you might be an introvert. You'd rather have one or two close friends than a whole bunch. You might shy away from being the captain of a team, but that doesn't mean that you don't want to play a sport. You can be pretty chatty once you get to know people. And even though you don't like to stand out, you aren't afraid to stand up for what you believe in.

11–20 Bubbles
You go with THE FLOW.

If you're comfortable meeting new people but still nervous about things like speaking in public, you might be an ambivert—and you're in good company. In a 2013 study, about two-thirds of the participants didn't fall into the introvert or extrovert category. They were somewhere in between. That might mean that one night you can hang for hours by yourself painting or reading a book, but the next night you're happy to go to a party.

21–30 Bubbles
You're a SOCIAL BUTTERFLY.

If you thrive around other people and love being the center of attention, you might be an extrovert. You prefer to talk to people face-to-face, and you're not afraid to share your feelings or even argue with somebody. Your friends see you as someone who is friendly, positive, and entertaining. You like to lead, though sometimes you might speak or act before you think.

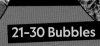

ARE YOU READY FOR
AN ADVENTURE?

Imagine that National Geographic is putting together a team of explorers to travel to some of the most exciting places in the world. We need you for our team—but what role will you have? All potential team members will go through an expedition training course in the Amazon rainforest. Answer the questions to take part in this training exercise, and then add up your results!

1. How will you train for the expedition?
    a. lifting weights
    b. hiking in the wilderness
    c. doing a mix of cardio and muscle training
    d. walking my dog

2. What do you want to learn from this expedition?
    a. I'd like to learn more about my teammates.
    b. I'd like to discover a place nobody has ever seen before.
    c. I'd like to learn traditional medicine from the local people.
    d. I'd like to learn more about animals that I've never seen before.

3. Which tool will you choose for your backpack?
    a. an emergency flare
    b. a GPS device
    c. a first aid kit
    d. binoculars

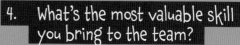

4. What's the most valuable skill you bring to the team?
    a. I don't fold under pressure.
    b. I know how to get around.
    c. I'm a caring person.
    d. I'm a good researcher.

5. The training director tells you that your goal is to travel through a section of the Amazon rainforest for 48 hours and record the animals you see. What are you most excited about?
    a. the chance to test my survival skills
    b. trying out my new GPS equipment
    c. using my skills to help the team
    d. seeing wildlife up close

6. The expedition begins. You and the team enter the rainforest when you hear a rustling sound nearby. It's a jaguar! What's your first instinct?

a. get the team to safety
b. find a different route through the rainforest
c. check the area to make sure the jaguar didn't injure anyone
d. photograph it

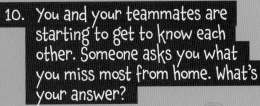

7. The jaguar moves on and your team does, too. It starts to rain. What's your first thought?

a. Will the rain slow our progress?
b. How can I protect my electronic equipment?
c. Everyone needs to watch their step on this slippery terrain.
d. It's the wet season! Maybe I'll see a migratory turtle.

8. One of your teammates slips on the wet ground and hurts an ankle. What do you do?

a. quickly order the team to work together to get the injured teammate to safety
b. locate the nearest medical center
c. perform temporary first aid
d. offer moral support

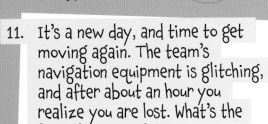

9. You set up camp as your teammate's ankle is being bandaged. While your team member rests, what do you read around the campfire?

a. a book about the history of Brazil
b. a map of the Amazon rainforest
c. an article about toxic plants in the rainforest
d. a book about toucans

10. You and your teammates are starting to get to know each other. Someone asks you what you miss most from home. What's your answer?

a. my family
b. my town
c. everything!
d. my pets

11. It's a new day, and time to get moving again. The team's navigation equipment is glitching, and after about an hour you realize you are lost. What's the first thing you do?

a. tell everyone not to panic
b. pull out my trusty compass
c. check my supplies of food and water
d. get distracted by the call of a bird overhead

12. The glitch is fixed, and you're back on track. Suddenly you spot a beautiful little golden frog. What do you do?

a. order the team to stop and observe it
b. plot my next move while the team studies the frog
c. warn everyone not to touch it—it could be poisonous!
d. confirm that it's poisonous but it's OK to observe

Continued ...

13. You see a harpy eagle hopping from branch to branch. What's your favorite fact about this species?

- **a.** They are the largest raptors in the rainforest.
- **b.** They have excellent eyesight.
- **c.** They can survive in dense rainforests, where other eagles can't.
- **d.** There are programs in place to protect their habitat.

14. You come to a river that you need to cross, and you see a school of piranhas. Your guidebook tells you they likely won't harm swimmers if they are not hungry. What do you do?

- **a.** I volunteer to wade into the river first.
- **b.** I plot a new route so we don't have to cross the river.
- **c.** I get my medical kit ready in case somebody gets hurt.
- **d.** I jump in! I want to brag that I've swum with piranhas!

15. You make it safely across the river. You're supposed to head east, but in the west you see a small village. What do you do?

- **a.** I insist that the team stick to the original mission.
- **b.** I offer to reroute the trip if everyone wants to explore the village.
- **c.** I worry that it's not safe to go off course.
- **d.** I try to convince everyone to keep looking for animals.

16. You continue into the dense forest and, without warning, a snake drops from a tree branch right in front of you. What do you do?

- **a.** I stand between my teammates and the snake.
- **b.** I run!
- **c.** I reach for a vial of anti-venom in case someone gets bitten.
- **d.** I assure everyone that I'm sure it's a common tree boa, and not venomous.

17. The trail takes you to another leg of the river. A pink river dolphin sticks its head out of the water. The team argues about whether to make camp and study it, or proceed to the end of the mission. What's your opinion?

- **a.** I want to proceed to the end of the mission as directed.
- **b.** I'd like to follow the dolphin and see where it goes.
- **c.** I remind everyone that we have limited survival gear.
- **d.** I vote for studying the dolphin for a few days.

18. You follow the river to the end of the expedition. A giant anteater crosses your path. What's your first thought?

- **a.** I hope the director is pleased with how many animals we've seen.
- **b.** I wonder where it's going.
- **c.** Does it bite?
- **d.** I'm so psyched that I got to see a giant anteater in its natural habitat!

19. You make it to the end of the training exercise! You and your teammates have really bonded on this trip. One of them gives you a nickname. What is it?

- **a.** Boss
- **b.** Captain
- **c.** Doc
- **d.** Professor

20. Where do you hope this experience will lead you 15 years from now?

- **a.** I'd like to be a ship's captain.
- **b.** It would be cool to be the voice of a GPS system.
- **c.** I want to work in a hospital.
- **d.** I'd be so happy working in a zoo.

IF YOU CHOSE MOSTLY ...

A's ... You're the **team leader.**

Your test results show that you have the ability to think clearly under pressure and to keep your emotions under control. Those are good qualities for a leader. But most important, you care about your teammates and their safety.

B's... You're the **navigator.**

You already have basic skills in reading a map and using a GPS system, and after the training we give you, you'll be able to navigate your teammates through any terrain.

C's... You're the **medic.**

You have the caring personality, and the ability to make quick decisions, that every medic needs. We'll equip you with the training and the equipment you need to handle minor medical emergencies.

D's... You're the **animal expert.**

You are fascinated by the amazing variety of living creatures on the planet, and you love to study them. On missions, you'll brief teams about local wildlife and get a chance to observe animals in their natural surroundings—something you've always dreamed of doing.

WHICH **DINOSAUR** ARE YOU?

FLOW-CHART

Imagine you're a dinosaur. What's the best way to survive?

Getting enough to eat

What do you eat?

Plants

What helps you eat a lot of plants?

Animals

How do you get enough animals to eat?

I'm good at catching my food.

Why are you good at catching your food?

I eat animals that nobody else does.

» YOU'RE A *SPINOSAURUS.*

This North African dinosaur is believed to be the only dinosaur that hunted in water, so it had plenty of fish to eat. A large "sail" on its back made of seven-foot (2-m) spines helped it survive.

Having protection from predators

What's the best way to protect yourself from predators?

Avoid them

Wear armor

Is armor all you need?

» YOU'RE A *PTERODACTYL.*

Winged reptiles such as the *ptero-dactyl* could fly away from land-dwelling carnivores. With wingspans ranging from six to 36 feet (2 to 11 m), they are the largest known flying animals in history. And while they were technically lizards, not dinosaurs, these high-flying reptiles lived during the same time period.

No

» YOU'RE AN EDMONTONIA.

The 22-foot (6.7-m)-long body of this Canadian herbivore was protected by bony armor. Sharp spikes on its body gave it added extra protection.

Yes

» YOU'RE A TRICERATOPS.

This dinosaur could eat any variety of plant, no matter how tough it was, thanks to its sharp beak. Then, it used its 800 tiny teeth to break the plant down.

» YOU'RE AN ANKYLOSAURUS.

Like *Edmontonia*, *Ankylosaurus* had bony plates and spikes for protection. It also had a clublike tail that could be used for whacking attackers.

My sharp teeth

My long neck

» YOU'RE AN APATOSAURUS.

The long neck of this herbivore would have allowed it to eat leaves from the very tops of trees, where others couldn't reach, or munch on plants very low to the ground.

I'm faster than my prey.

» YOU'RE A VELOCIRAPTOR.

This dinosaur used its incredible speed and agility to survive. It could chase down small plant-eating dinosaurs and then attack them with the sickle-shaped sharp claws on the bottom of its feet.

I'm powerful.

» YOU'RE A TYRANNOSAURUS REX.

This dinosaur's strong head, neck, and jaws allowed it to latch on to smaller dinosaurs. *T. rex* could eat 500 pounds (230 kg) of meat in one bite!

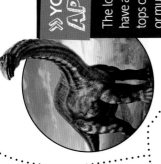

COULD YOU SURVIVE ON A DESERTED ISLAND?

You're stranded on a tropical island with only a suitcase full of your stuff. Could you survive? Count each statement you agree with to see if you'd be right at home—or if you'd need immediate rescue.

- I have caught a fish.
- I have cleaned and cooked a fish that I've caught.
- I love the feel of sand between my toes.
- I am a good swimmer.
- I know how to stay calm in an emergency.
- I have spent more than 24 hours without touching a cell phone.

- I know how to start a fire without matches.
- Finding freshwater is the first thing you should do if you are stranded.
- It doesn't bother me to spend long periods of time alone.

- I know how to make my own food.
- I have gone on a camping trip.
- I am a member of the Girl Scouts or Boy Scouts.
- I never go anywhere without a compass.
- I have slept underneath the stars.
- I have used a hammer.
- It's important to stay in the shade when the sun is hot.
- I don't need a soft bed to sleep on.
- I get at least 5,000 steps in every day.

- Survival shows are the only shows I watch on TV.

- Sure, I'd eat a bug!

- I have read the book *Hatchet*.

- Somebody's trash is someone else's treasure.

- I have cracked open a coconut.

- I once helped build a tree house.

- When things get tough, I stay positive.

Point Nemo, the most remote spot on Earth, is farther from land in any direction than the International Space Station is from Earth.

- I know how to whittle wood.

- I can row a boat.

- I know how to entertain myself.

- I don't get cranky when I get hungry.

- I know which plants and fungi are edible and which are poisonous.

IF YOU COUNTED ...

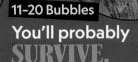

1–10 Bubbles
You'll need
IMMEDIATE RESCUE.

It takes a very special set of skills to survive on a deserted island, and your strengths are in other areas. To survive the elements, you'll need to know a few basics. Your focus should be to find freshwater, create a shelter, and make a fire. Then, find some way to make a rescue signal. Write in big letters in the sand, or spell out your message in large rocks. Then cross your fingers that you'll be found and rescued soon!

11–20 Bubbles
You'll probably
SURVIVE.

You've likely been camping or spent time outdoors swimming and fishing, and those skills will help you survive for a while. You have some idea of how to make a shelter, and you can probably make a decent fire. But being alone might be a challenge for you, so you'll have to work to keep up your spirits. Don't forget to make a rescue signal, because you might not have enough skills to dig in your heels for the long haul.

21–30 Bubbles
You'll
THRIVE!

If for some reason you do get stranded on a deserted island, you'll probably do great. Based on your answers, it's like you've been preparing your whole life for it. You love watching survival shows and taking survival courses such as edible plant identification. That means you know the rules of survival, and how important it is to use everything in your surroundings—even trash that washes up on the beach—to help you. You don't mind being alone, and you can stay calm and positive when things get tough.

WHICH OCEAN CAREER IS FOR YOU?

1. How deep do you want to go?
- **a.** I'd like to stick close to the surface.
- **b.** Deeper than the surface, but not too deep!
- **c.** Far enough to see some deep-sea creatures.
- **d.** Take me to the ocean floor!

2. What would you do if you spotted a shark swimming next to your boat?
- **a.** capture it, tag it, and release it so I can study it
- **b.** hang out in a shark-proof cage and film the shark
- **c.** avoid it
- **d.** ignore it

3. Pick a place to explore:
- **a.** a shoreline full of penguins
- **b.** a coral reef
- **c.** a shipwreck
- **d.** an undersea volcano

4. Pick a school subject:
- **a.** biology
- **b.** drama
- **c.** history
- **d.** geology

IF YOU CHOSE MOSTLY ...

A's... Marine biologist

You're fascinated with animals and would love to study their behavior up close, so you might want to become a scientist who studies animals that live in salt water. There are many different career paths marine biologists can take. They can study tiny plankton with a microscope, help track polar bears in the Arctic, or take care of creatures in aquariums and zoos.

B's... Underwater filmmaker

You're a visual person who believes the ocean has stories to tell, so you might want to become an underwater filmmaker. These filmmakers collect images of the underwater world that appear in books, films, magazines, and TV shows. They dive into places no one has gone before to get their footage. This career will take you to ocean environments all around the world, from colorful coral reefs in the tropics to icebergs in the Antarctic.

5. Pick an ocean animal:

a. sea lion

b. great white shark

c. barracuda

d. anglerfish

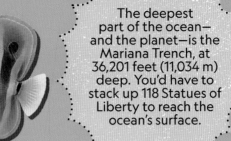

The deepest part of the ocean—and the planet—is the Mariana Trench, at 36,201 feet (11,034 m) deep. You'd have to stack up 118 Statues of Liberty to reach the ocean's surface.

6. Pick an activity on land:

a. visit a zoo

b. go to the movies

c. go to a museum

d. climb a mountain

7. What do you want to do with your career?

a. help

b. tell stories

c. discover

d. explore

8. Pick a piece of equipment:

a. scuba gear

b. underwater video camera

c. sonar scanner

d. remotely operated underwater vehicle

9. Which word best describes you?

a. studious

b. entertaining

c. curious

d. adventurous

10. Where would you like to go on vacation?

a. Seal Island National Wildlife Refuge in Maine

b. an underwater hotel in Tanzania

c. a tour of ancient buildings in Greece

d. Mauna Loa volcano in Hawaii

C's... Marine archaeologist

Your love of learning about the past makes you a good candidate for this career. On land, archaeologists dig through dirt to find clues about the past—and marine archaeologists do the same thing underwater. They search for clues about how humans in the past used the oceans and what their lives were like. They find these clues on shipwrecks, or in sunken towns, docks, or dwellings.

D's... Geological oceanographer

You know that the ocean floor is ripe for discovery and exploration, and you're daring enough to want to explore it. Like you, geological oceanographers are fascinated by what's happening on the ocean floor. They map the terrain and provide data that can help predict earthquakes and tsunamis. Their explorations can take them to the ocean's deepest trenches and to the ridges of undersea volcanoes.

WHICH AUSTRALIAN ANIMAL ARE YOU?

What's for lunch?

I think I'll just have a salad.

After lunch, want to go outside?

Can we stay inside?

Sure!

Should we go for a jog or hang out in a tree house?

Let's go for a jog.

» YOU'RE A RED KANGAROO.

You'd have to be pretty speedy to keep up with a red kangaroo—it can run faster than 35 miles an hour (56 km/h). Its speed helps it avoid human and dingo predators.

Some fish might be nice.

Do you usually make jokes, or laugh at other people's jokes?

Other people make me laugh.

I make jokes.

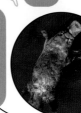

» YOU'RE A PLATYPUS.

You make people smile with your jokes, and this mammal makes people smile with its unusual appearance. The platypus looks like a duck wearing a fur coat!

A juicy burger

Will you eat with your family, or alone?

I'll eat with my family.

I'll eat by myself, thanks.

» YOU'RE A DINGO.

Like the dingo, you're usually not found alone. These wild dogs roam Australia in packs, hunting for wallabies, rodents, rabbits, and birds to eat.

Let's hang out in a tree house!

YOU'RE A KOALA.

These mammals like to spend time in trees, too, to stay safe from predators. Their favorite food: eucalyptus leaves. Most creatures can't eat the toxic leaves, but koalas have special bacteria in their stomachs that help them digest it.

Sure, let's talk. What's your best feature?

My impressive ears

YOU'RE A BILBY.

Your ears might not look like rabbit ears, but the bilby's do, which is why people call this animal Australia's Easter Bunny. Its ears help it listen for insects underground.

My strong hands

YOU'RE A KOOKABURRA.

If you've got a loud, rowdy laugh, you'd fit right into a kookaburra clan! This bird's call sounds like human laughter.

YOU'RE A WOMBAT.

Bearlike in appearance, this animal lives in the ground and uses its shovel-like front paws to dig tunnels. They sleep in these burrows during the day.

My teeth. In fact, that salad didn't satisfy me. I'd like to chomp down on a burger right now.

YOU'RE A TASMANIAN DEVIL.

You don't mind being alone, like this marsupial, which usually lives on its own in hollow logs, caves, or under-ground burrows. This meat-eating member of the kangaroo's family has large teeth made for dining on animals such as wallabies and possums.

WHICH ANCIENT CIVILIZATION WOULD YOU HAVE FIT INTO?

Have you ever wondered how you would have fared during a time without cell phones and electricity? Take this quiz to see which of these ancient civilizations you might have felt at home in.

1. Choose a way to get around:

a. rowboat
b. canoe
c. sailboat
d. chariot

2. What's for dinner?

a. lentils with garlic
b. corn and beans
c. bread, cheese, and olives
d. fish and rice

3. What can't you live without?

a. books
b. chocolate
c. my alarm clock
d. noodles

4. Choose a precious material:

a. lapis lazuli
b. jade
c. diamond
d. bronze

5. Choose an animal:

a. crocodile
b. dog
c. snake
d. tiger

6. How would you spend a day off?

a. writing in my journal
b. playing sports
c. going for a run
d. flying a kite

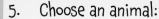

7. Choose an emoji:

a.

b.

c.

d.

8. Which subject interests you most?

a. medicine
b. astronomy
c. music
d. mathematics

9. Choose a fruit:

a. melon
b. papaya
c. apricot
d. grapes

10. Choose an environment:

a. desert
b. rainforest
c. mountain
d. bamboo forest

11. Choose an art form:

a. mural painting
b. stone carvings
c. marble sculpture
d. fabric making

IF YOU CHOSE MOSTLY ...

A's... Ancient Egypt (3150–30 B.C.)

This civilization might allow you to explore your love of writing. If you were lucky (and male), you might have become a scribe. Or you might have farmed on the banks of the Nile River, playing board games, swimming, and dancing in your spare time. If you were less lucky, you would have done backbreaking labor for the pharaoh—who might have been female, because ancient Egypt had more women rulers than anywhere else on Earth.

B's... Ancient Maya (1800 B.C.–A.D. 900)

You like the idea of eating tropical foods and studying the night sky, so you might fit in the Maya civilization, which thrived in what is modern-day Central America. Life for most ancient Maya was hard work. Many worked hard farming. But you'd have plenty of corn and beans to eat, and maybe even some chocolate. If you could become a Mayan priest, you'd study the sun, stars, and planets in observatories.

C's... Ancient Greece (1200–323 B.C.)

You'd like to live someplace warm and sunny, with art and music to enjoy, and ancient Greece might fit the bill. As in most ancient civilizations, life was better here if you were a boy, because—unlike girls—you could go to school and learn about math, reading, writing, and music. And thanks to ancient Greek advances in medicine, you might have survived if you got sick or hurt.

D's... The Shang dynasty (1600–1046 B.C.)

If you're a fan of food and beauty, you might want to live here, in the first recorded dynasty in China. In this time period, people wove silk and brewed tea. You might have learned to make music with chimes made of stone. Scholars today learn about the Shang from the tombs they left behind, filled with bronze objects and animals carved in jade.

CHOOSE
Night Owl OR *Early Bird?*

Daylight is overrated.

Watch your mouth!

The term "night owl" is used for people who like to stay up late, because most owls are nocturnal—active at night, and asleep during the day.

IF YOU CHOSE *This:*

Who needs an alarm clock? Not you! You pop out of bed like bread from a toaster every morning. The saying goes that "the early bird gets the worm," and early risers get a lot of other benefits, too. Waking up early gives you more time to plan or exercise before you start your day. And a study at the University of North Texas in 2008 showed that students who reported being more active in the morning got better grades than those who didn't. So if you like to rise and shine, you'll get your day—and maybe even your life—off to a great start!

Early Bird

Night Owl

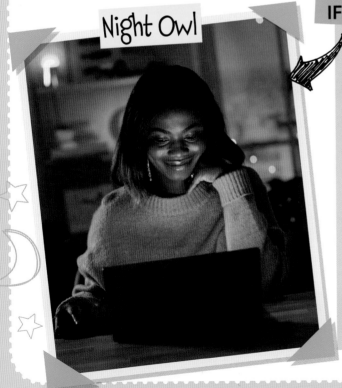

IF YOU CHOSE *That:*

Night owls generally like to stay up late—and sleep in whenever they can. Sometimes they get a bad rap for not being go-getters, but there's evidence that there are benefits to being a night owl as well. A study in Milan found that people who stayed up late were good at coming up with creative solutions to problems, and some think that it's because the quiet and peace of nighttime make it easier to be creative. Also, night owls can soar to great heights: In 2009, President Barack Obama said that he was a night owl and stayed up past midnight every night!

WHICH NATURAL WONDER SHOULD YOU VISIT?

There are some spots in the world that are famous for their breathtaking natural beauty. If you could go on an expedition to one of these wonders, which one would it be?

1. Which country would you like to explore?
- **a.** U.S.A.
- **b.** Mexico
- **c.** Iceland
- **d.** Zimbabwe

2. Which outdoor activity would you like to try?
- **a.** camping
- **b.** hiking
- **c.** stargazing
- **d.** safari

3. Which animal would you love to photograph in the wild?
- **a.** cougar
- **b.** armadillo
- **c.** arctic fox
- **d.** giraffe

4. Which of these foods would you like to try on your expedition?
- **a.** veggie sandwich and granola bar
- **b.** spicy meat stew
- **c.** black licorice ice cream
- **d.** wild mushroom soup

IF YOU CHOSE MOSTLY ...

A's ... The Grand Canyon

You're not afraid to rough it, especially if the adventure comes with an amazing view. You can hike and camp inside this canyon in Arizona, U.S.A., getting a close-up view of rocky peaks and deep gorges. Or take a thrilling raft ride through the canyon, down the Colorado River.

B's ... The Parícutin Volcano

You're up for a hike and hope to see some animals while you're doing it. This Mexican volcano is one of the youngest in the world, and modern scientists got to watch it grow. It erupted out of the ground in 1943, and then grew to 1,475 feet (450 meters) tall in its first year. You can hike up the volcano just about any time, and if you're there in the fall, you can travel nearby to watch monarch butterflies return from the north.

5. What do you want to get out of your trip?

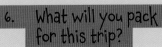

a. I want to sleep under the stars.

b. I want to be inspired by nature.

c. I want to see something really beautiful.

d. I want to see wild animals.

6. What will you pack for this trip?

a. tent

b. hiking shoes

c. telescope

d. binoculars

7. What else do you want to do before you go home?

a. go river rafting

b. see the migration of monarch butterflies

c. watch a geothermal geyser erupt

d. bungee jump from a bridge

8. What's your best quality?

a. I'm energetic.

b. I love animals.

c. I'm curious.

d. I'm daring.

9. A natural wonder should be ...

a. big!

b. historic.

c. colorful.

d. breathtaking.

10. What souvenir do you want to bring back with you?

a. handmade wood carving

b. T-shirt with a volcano design

c. tin of dried fish

d. elephant plushie

C's... The Northern Lights

You don't mind the cold and aren't looking for a physical challenge—just some beautiful sights. Iceland is a great place to see this stunning light show, which streaks the night sky with fluorescent colors. While you're in Iceland, you can visit geysers, glaciers, hot springs, and Viking ruins—and eat some fish dishes you've probably never had before—including fermented shark.

D's... Victoria Falls

Your adventurous spirit would love to explore this waterfall, which descends 355 feet (108 m) and is part of the Zambezi River on the border between Zambia and Zimbabwe. While many know it as Victoria Falls, after Queen Victoria, the Indigenous people call it Mosi-oa-Tunya, which means "the smoke that thunders." The falls are close to grasslands that are home to wildlife such as giraffes, elephants, and zebras. Daredevils love to bungee jump over the Zambezi River, launching off a bridge alongside the falls.

CHECKLIST CHALLENGE

HOW SILLY ARE YOU?

Do you walk through life in sensible shoes—or glittery light-up sneakers? Count each statement you agree with to find out how serious or silly you are.

- ○ I have squirted liquid out of my nose while laughing.

- ○ I have competed in an ugly sweater contest.

- ○ Laughter is the best medicine.

- ○ I can speak fluent Pig Latin.

- ○ I know how to juggle.

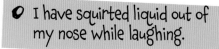

- ○ Nobody tells a knock-knock joke like I do.

- ○ I watch more than three hours of cartoons a week.

- ○ Why walk when you can skip?

- ○ April Fool's Day is my favorite holiday.

- ○ I have a better imagination than most people.

- ○ I always win at charades.

- ○ My socks almost never match.

- ○ There is nothing wrong with pineapple on pizza.

- ○ Every year I dress up my pet in a Halloween costume.

- ○ I wish every day was Inside-Out Day.

- ○ When I eat, I make noises so it sounds like my food is screaming.

- ○ I'd love to have a pet chicken that I could bring to school with me.

- ○ Clowns are the best part of a circus.

- ○ Sometimes I daydream about riding a unicorn.

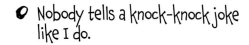

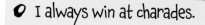

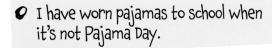

- I'm good at making my friends laugh.

- I stick googly eyes to ordinary household objects.

- When I make pancakes, I use chocolate chips to make smiley faces on them.

- Bubble Wrap was made for popping.

- I love that video of the squirrel on water skis.

- I have worn pajamas to school when it's not Pajama Day.

- Finger painting is my favorite form of artistic expression.

- I don't fight with my friends often, but when I do, it's a pillow fight!

- I have eaten ice cream for breakfast.

- Why walk around puddles when you can splash in them?

- I know you are, but what am I?

IF YOU COUNTED ...

1–10 Bubbles
You are
PRETTY SERIOUS.

You usually take things seriously—but that doesn't mean you don't like to have fun! If someone makes you a smiley-faced pancake you'll smile back, and you'll participate in silly days at school, like Inside-Out Day, because you like to follow the rules. But you are a no-nonsense person who doesn't like distractions when something needs to get done. Your friends appreciate that you take them seriously.

11–20 Bubbles
You are
SOMEWHAT SILLY.

You know when to be silly—like at a birthday party—and you know when to be serious, like in the library. You probably have a few silly skills up your sleeve, too—maybe you're good at telling jokes, or you can balance things on your nose. You are silly enough to enjoy a good pillow fight, but definitely not silly enough to skip everywhere you go. That's a good mix.

21–30 Bubbles
You are
SERIOUSLY SILLY!

Ice cream for breakfast? Sure! And who cares if your socks don't match? There's only one thing you're really serious about—making people laugh. You crack up your friends with your jokes and the way you play with your food in the cafeteria. You take the time to learn complicated silly tricks, such as juggling, and look forward to showing them off. Your favorite day of the year is probably April Fool's Day, when you plan elaborate pranks for your friends and family.

WHAT KIND OF FRIEND ARE YOU?

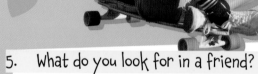

1. Your friend texts you: "Want to hang out?" What do you reply?

a. I'll be right over!

b. Honestly, I'm not in the mood. Maybe tomorrow?

c. Sure. What would you like to do?

d. I'm already outside!

2. It's your friend's birthday. What do you do?

a. I throw him a surprise party!

b. I get him a nice card.

c. I bake him a batch of his favorite cookies.

d. I help him plan his birthday party.

3. It's your birthday, and your friend forgot. What do you do?

a. I text her "Happy Birthday to ME!"

b. I call and tell her it hurt my feelings.

c. I tell her it's my birthday and invite her over.

d. I mark my calendar so I won't forget *her* birthday.

4. How many friends do you have?

a. Let me think ... at least 10!

b. That's none of your business.

c. I have a small group of close friends.

d. I have one best friend.

5. What do you look for in a friend?

a. someone who laughs at my jokes

b. someone who tells the truth

c. someone who cares as much for me as I do for them

d. someone who will always have my back

6. It's Saturday! What will you do with your friend?

a. We'll go to the mall.

b. We'll stay home where other people won't bother us.

c. I'll help my friend babysit his little brother and sister.

d. We'll get matching haircuts.

7. How would you show a friend that you care?

a. I'd decorate her locker at school.

b. I'd text her and let her know.

c. I'd help her with homework.

d. I'd make a scrapbook with my favorite photos of us.

8. You have two tickets to a concert, but two of your friends want to go with you. What do you do?

 a. I forget the concert and invite my friends over to blast music at home.
 b. I choose one friend to go with me, and tell the other one they're out.
 c. I give my friends the tickets so both can go without me.
 d. I find some way to get another ticket so all three of us can go.

9. Your friend says something that hurts your feelings. What do you do?

 a. I laugh and tell my friend to chill out.
 b. I tell him he hurt my feelings and I need some time to get over it.
 c. I cry but don't tell my friend what's bothering me.
 d. We talk it out.

10. Your friend asks you to try out for the school musical with her, but you don't really want to. What do you do?

 a. I like painting, so I offer to work on the sets instead.
 b. I tell her I don't want to.
 c. I tell her I'm too shy, but I offer to help her memorize her lines.
 d. I practice singing and dancing so I can get a part in the musical, too.

IF YOU CHOSE MOSTLY ...

A's... You're a fun friend.

You love to make your friends laugh, and you're the best at cheering up your friends when they're down. Your outgoing personality means that you probably have more friends than you can count.

B's... You're a frank friend.

The word "frank" means "honest," and you are a friend who tells it like it is. You despise lies and secrets, and you'd rather tell your friend the truth about how you're feeling, even if it stings a little. Your friends appreciate you because they know you'll always be straight with them.

C's... You're a feeling friend.

You're a very compassionate person, and you like to take care of your friends. You're the friend who remembers every special occasion and knows everything your friends love to eat and what music they like. You're a helpful friend who always offers a hand when your friend needs one.

D's... You're a faithful friend.

You believe that loyalty is important, and any friend of yours knows that you will always be there for them, no matter what. You probably have one or two close friends instead of a big group of them, but for you, quality is important, not quantity. When you become friends with someone, you will be their friend for life.

WHICH **GEMSTONE** ARE YOU?

What's your ideal temperature?

I like it cool.

I like it hot.

Are you a smooth talker or rough around the edges?

What's more important—great skills or good looks?

I'm a smooth talker.

I'm a little rough around the edges.

Would you rather chill out or have an adventure?

Do you prefer daytime or nighttime?

I love the quiet darkness of the night.

Chill out

I love the sunshine!

Would you rather wear purple or pink?

Purple

» YOU'RE PEARL.

Smooth and shiny, the more perfectly sphere-shaped a pearl is, the more valuable it is. Like a pearl, you are admired for your grace and beauty.

» YOU'RE OBSIDIAN.

When hot lava cools, it can form this dark black natural glass. People find peace in obsidian—and in your soothing, cool personality..

» YOU'RE AMETHYST.

It's a form of quartz, and some feel that it has a soothing, calming effect on those who wear it. You have that same effect on the people in your life.

Good looks

Great skills

Would you rather read a mystery novel or watch a funny movie?

Which of these qualities do you think is your strongest?

Read a mystery novel

Watch a funny movie

I'm powerful.

»YOU'RE PERIDOT.

These stones are found in unusual places—volcanic rocks and meteorites. Your curious nature is a good match for this mysterious gem.

»YOU'RE CITRINE.

The word "citrine" has the same origin as the French word for "lemon," and like a citrine, you are known for cheering up those around you with your fresh, sunny personality and your zest for life!

»YOU'RE A RUBY.

Prized for their intense red color, rubies were worn in the crowns of kings and in the swords of warriors. Your leadership skills shine as brightly as a ruby red jewel.

I'm tough.

Have an adventure!

»YOU'RE AQUAMARINE.

The name of this gem means "water of the sea," and according to lore it brought fishermen good luck. You are as spirited and adventurous as a sea-going sailor.

»YOU'RE A DIAMOND.

The hardest natural substance on Earth, diamonds are prized for their strength as well as their beauty. When things get tough, you don't back down.

I'm loyal.

Pink

I'm compassionate.

»YOU'RE ROSE QUARTZ.

The pale pink color of this gem is associated with love and kindness. People feel comfortable around your gentle spirit.

»YOU'RE A SAPPHIRE.

With a deep blue color that comes from iron and titanium, sapphires sometimes symbolize loyalty. Your friends know you are someone they can count on.

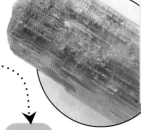

Thomas Edison

ARE YOU MORE LIKE

OR Nikola Tesla?

Their styles of working, thinking, and creating were very different. Yet at the turn of the 20th century, Edison and Tesla each discovered a way to generate electricity—and they waged a feud over whose method would one day be used around the world. Which of these innovators are you most like? To find out, decide if each statement below is true or false, and keep track of your answers.

TRUE OR FALSE

It's better to be practical than creative.

Thinking is good, but you need to experiment to really test something.

I'd rather have a small idea succeed than have a big idea fail.

I think it would be fun to be famous.

I think I'll probably get married someday.

I'm popular.

If you want to succeed, get some enemies.

Doing is better than dreaming.

Genius is one percent inspiration and 99 percent perspiration.

I don't think I'd look good with a mustache.

Inventions should solve problems that people have.

If at first you don't succeed, try, try again.

I am not a very good organizer.

I like to tinker with things.

I can be awkward in social situations.

I am not afraid of germs.

I'd rather have good skills than big ideas.

I like to boss other people around.

Other people wish they could be like me.

If I do something awesome, I'll brag about it.

Math is not my best subject.

I am a good problem solver.

There's no point in inventing something if you can't make money from it.

When I succeed at something, I tell everyone about it.

I would rather work with a team than work by myself.

My friends say I am fun to be around.

I don't let my weaknesses stop me from succeeding.

I think I'd be good at running a business.

IF YOU CHOSE MOSTLY ...

False ... You're more like *Nikola Tesla.*

You have big ideas and visions, just like this Serbian American inventor. He dreamed of producing free energy for everyone in the world. Some of his big ideas led to real-life inventions, such as a system of transmitting electricity, and he even designed a hydroelectric power plant at Niagara Falls. Other big ideas stayed in his notebooks, or were never finished. He might not have had Edison's success during his lifetime, but since his death in 1943, he has become a legend. Scientists continued to study his research, and in 2003, the Tesla electric vehicle company was named after him.

True ... You're more like *Thomas Edison.*

You believe in getting things right, no matter how many tries it takes. This hardworking inventor put together a team of scientists in Menlo Park, New Jersey, U.S.A., to help him test his ideas again and again until he got results. He ended up with 1,093 patents in his name for inventions such as the phonograph, microphone, and electric generator. He believed in coming up with inventions that would solve problems—and then sold them to the highest bidder. He had a big personality, was exciting to be around, and loved to brag about his success.

HOW WILL YOU BECOME FAMOUS?

Do you dream of achieving something so amazing that the world knows your name? Do you practice signing your autograph just in case someone asks for it? If so, you want to be famous. There's no one formula that will guarantee you fame—but this quiz might give you a clue about what road you should take to get there.

1. **What does the world need more of?**
   a. ways for people to be heard
   b. entertainment
   c. clean air and water
   d. laughter

2. **Where do you shine?**
   a. on the debate team
   b. on stage
   c. organizing a roadside cleanup
   d. on social media

3. **What makes you happy?**
   a. reaching a goal
   b. performing
   c. helping people
   d. just being myself

4. **Pick an emoji:**
   a.
   b.
   c.
   d.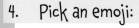

5. **Would you like to dance?**
   a. Sure, as long as the cameras are on.
   b. Not until I have a few more years of lessons.
   c. How can anyone dance when the world is in danger?
   d. Yes! I record myself dancing all the time.

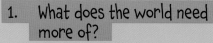

6. I wish that I could be more ...
a. convincing.
b. perfect.
c. courageous.
d. confident.

7. If I become famous, my crew will include ...
a. my campaign manager.
b. my makeup artist.
c. a documentary filmmaker.
d. my best friends.

8. My dream dwelling is ...
a. a small house with a white picket fence in front.
b. a California beach house.
c. a yurt.
d. an arcade filled with my favorite games.

9. It's lunchtime.
a. I'm serving food at a local homeless shelter.
b. I'm performing at an assisted living center while the residents eat.
c. I'm eating a salad that I grew myself.
d. I'm making sure my food looks great so I can take a photo of it.

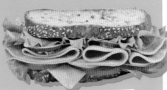

10. The best thing about being famous is ...
a. being able to influence people.
b. the energy of my fans fuels my creativity.
c. it helps me get the word out.
d. I'm not sure. It's actually kind of embarrassing.

IF YOU CHOSE MOSTLY ...

A's ... You'll **win an election.**

You are a politician at heart, and you think the best way to make a change in the world is to work within the system. You already know that a sure way to win over the people is to be friendly and relatable, and to have a strong argument.

B's ... You'll **star in a movie.**

You are a performer, and you know that if you work really hard at your craft, you might get discovered one day. Then again, you might not. In the field of acting, luck is as important as acting lessons. (Some famous actors, including megastar Tom Cruise, never went to acting school!)

C's ... You'll **fight for the planet.**

You will join the ranks of Greta Thunberg and try to get world leaders to pay attention to the climate crisis. Or you might take up another cause, such as human rights. The important thing is you have a voice and you're not afraid to use it.

D's ... You'll **become a meme.**

Move over, Doug the Pug and Side-Eye Chloe! You'll most likely become famous as the subject of a meme or a viral video. Some social media celebs love the attention, and others wish they had never become famous. If you're not sure how you'd feel about it, then maybe think twice before posting yourself doing anything silly.

WHICH **STINKY ANIMAL** ARE YOU?

Why are you stinky?

I'm not stinky!

For protection

To get attention

I want to show that I belong.

Why do you need protection?

What are you trying to say?

» YOU'RE A HYENA.

Pack members excrete nasty-smelling "hyena butter" that communicates a unique family scent.

I'm slow.

I'm small.

Stay away from my territory!

» YOU'RE A SKUNK.

Skunks douse predators with stinky spray so they have time to run away and hide.

» YOU'RE A STINK BUG.

This little critter is so stinky, it was named for its stench! Its foul aroma helps keep the bug safe from predators.

» YOU'RE A WOLVERINE.

Wolverines use a smelly scent to mark their territory, keeping predators away from their food sources.

Are you sure?

Like a movie snack?

Yes! I smell great!

» YOU'RE A BINTURONG.

Humans say these catlike Asian forest dwellers smell like buttered popcorn!

Well, sometimes I'm a little smelly.

Yes, like popcorn.

Yes, like cherry cola.

» YOU'RE A SLOTH.

Algae and bugs live on the fur of these slow-moving mammals, creating a funky odor.

» YOU'RE A SPOTTED MILLIPEDE.

Under stress, this creature releases a chemical that some say smells just like cherry cola.

Like a cough drop?

Yes, like eucalyptus.

I'm better than you!

Yes, like lemon.

» YOU'RE A KOALA.

They smell minty and piney, just like the eucalyptus leaves they eat.

» YOU'RE A RING-TAILED LEMUR.

During mating season, males give off a foul odor to keep other males away from potential female partners. They hold "stink-offs" until one of them backs down.

» YOU'RE A CITRONELLA ANT.

They release a lemony-fresh scent when they're stepped on.

HOW
CURIOUS
ARE YOU?

Do you take life at face value or question everything? Count each statement that you agree with to find your curiosity quotient!

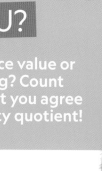

- I always read the last page of a book first.

- I have taken apart things just to see how they work.

- I check for spoilers before I go see a movie.

- I hate it when my friends keep secrets from me.

- At a museum, I take the time to read all the signs describing the displays.

- When I meet someone new, I look them up online right away.

- I like reading nonfiction better than fiction.

- A "Keep Out" sign is just a suggestion.

- I read or listen to news about current events every day.

- When I meet someone new, I ask them questions to learn more about them.

- My friends say I am a good listener.

- Sometimes I want to open mail that belongs to someone else in my home.

- Before I eat or drink something, I read the ingredients on the package.

- I would like to interview my grandparents to find out what their lives were like when they were young.

- I don't mind admitting when I am wrong.

- I prefer to take on one task at a time. I'm not a multitasker.

- I never get bored.

- I don't judge a book by its cover.

- I don't mind surprises.

- I don't give up easily.

- I like solving problems.

- I look forward to school most of the time.

- I'd rather go to the library than to the mall.

- I think that I'm a pretty creative person.

- When I read fiction, I read mostly mystery novels.

- When I get a gift, I shake the box to try to guess what's inside.

- I sometimes eavesdrop on other people's conversations.

- I like to know everything about my favorite celebrities.

- I never fall asleep in the middle of a movie.

- I like doing science experiments.

IF YOU COUNTED ...

1–10 Bubbles
You're mildly
SNOOPY.

You'd rather enjoy your cell phone than try to figure out how it works. You HATE movie spoilers. You are a good keeper of secrets, and you respect the privacy of others. These are good qualities, but you may want to think about exploring the things that interest you a little more. In 2013, a study at George Mason University showed that more curious people opened themselves up to more joy and discovery.

11–20 Bubbles
You're a
SLEUTH.

You have a curious nature, and you're very interested in the world around you. You don't get bored easily. When you meet new people, you ask them questions and show an interest in them. This leads them to want to learn more about you, and you can form deeper friendships this way. These traits mean you might make a great science researcher, police detective, or mystery novelist.

21–30 Bubbles
You're seriously
CURIOUS.

Being very curious is definitely something to celebrate. Research done at Harvard Business School in 2018 showed that curious people at work are usually great at creative problem-solving. But if you've ever heard the phrase "curiosity killed the cat," then you know there's a flip side to being too curious. Enjoy your curious nature, but be sure to respect boundaries. That'll keep you safe and keep others from being upset with you.

WHICH ANIMAL CAREER WOULD BE BEST FOR YOU?

Do you love animals and dream about working with them someday? Take this quiz to find out what interesting animal career might be up your alley.

1. **Which animal would you love to spend time with?**
   a. giraffe
   b. raccoon
   c. puppy
   d. rabbit

2. **I love animals because ...**
   a. we can learn so much from them.
   b. they're a vital part of the ecosystem.
   c. they're entertaining.
   d. they are great companions.

3. **My favorite way to experience animals is ...**
   a. at a zoo.
   b. out in nature.
   c. on video.
   d. to live with them.

4. **Which of these jobs working with humans would you like most?**
   a. chef
   b. athletic trainer
   c. kindergarten teacher
   d. guidance counselor

5. **Pick a vacation:**
   a. go on an African safari
   b. camp in a national park
   c. take a tour of Hollywood
   d. eat with kittens at a Tokyo cat café

6. **My friends say I am:**
   a. curious
   b. brave
   c. patient
   d. caring

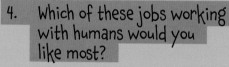
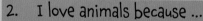

7. **The best thing you can do for an animal is ...**
   a. give it a safe place to live.
   b. help it when it's hurting.
   c. train it.
   d. rescue it.

8. **Which celebrity animal is your favorite?**
   a. Koko the gorilla
   b. Punxsutawney Phil the groundhog
   c. Babe the pig
   d. Toto from *The Wizard of Oz*

9. **Which of these statements is most true about you?**
   a. I like reading.
   b. I'm in tune with the natural world.
   c. I'm good at solving problems.
   d. I'm a good communicator.

10. **Pick a Saturday afternoon activity:**
    a. build a birdhouse
    b. hike through the woods
    c. go see a movie
    d. volunteer at my local hospital

IF YOU CHOSE MOSTLY ...

A's ... You could be a zoologist.

Your love of animals and desire to get closer to them might lead you to this career. A zoologist is a scientist who does everything from caring for animals to designing enclosures for them to teaching the public about them. Not every zoologist works in a zoo—you might end up in a university, an aquarium, a wildlife center, or a nature preserve. And others study animals where they live, the way Jane Goodall studied chimpanzees in Africa.

B's ... You could be a wildlife rehabilitator.

Your heart is drawn to furry woodland creatures and wild birds. When someone finds a small wild animal that has been injured—such as a squirrel or raccoon in North America—the animal is often brought to a wildlife rehabilitator. The rehabilitator is someone who has been trained to give wild animals basic care until they recover and can be released in the wild. They might also hand-raise baby animals that have lost their parents.

C's ... You could be an animal trainer.

You like having pets and learning how to train them. Professionals in this career do a wide range of training. Some train dogs or cats to obey commands and be good pets. Others train birds of prey to hunt with them, or teach dogs special tasks such as search and rescue or how to be a therapy dog. Others teach animals of all kinds to do tricks on command for movies and TV shows.

D's ... You could work in an animal shelter.

Your heart goes out to dogs, cats, and other pets that don't have homes. Besides taking care of rescued animals, animal shelter workers can also act as adoption counselors. They interview families who are interested in adopting pets, or help run websites that promote pets that are up for adoption. Some workers do this as a career, but all shelters use volunteers to help take dogs for walks, or even read to pets to keep them company.

WHO'S YOUR
ROBOT SIDEKICK?

Why do you want a sidekick?

I think I'd like a friend.

I want a sidekick that helps me help others.

Do you want a friend that looks human, or like a robot?

Who do you want to help?

The elderly

Like a human **Like a robot**

⟫ YOUR ROBOT SIDEKICK IS
ROMEO.

This robot is the size of a human. It can open doors for its elderly owners, help them climb stairs, and reach for objects for them.

What do you want to do with your friend?

Have you always wanted a dog?

Talk

Yes!

Not really

I don't know, maybe shoot some hoops?

⟫ YOUR ROBOT SIDEKICK IS
SPOT.

Boston Dynamics made this robot that can walk, trot, climb, and hop. Spot might not be cuddly, but he won't make a mess on your carpet, either.

Stay healthy

⟫ YOUR ROBOT SIDEKICK IS
SOPHIA.

This humanoid robot can have a conversation with you! She's even been on *The Tonight Show* and is an official citizen of Saudi Arabia.

⟫ YOUR ROBOT SIDEKICK IS
ZENBO.

You can listen to music or take photos with this cute robot, and Zenbo (from ASUS Robotics) can even tell you a story. Its facial display can show emotions, just like a human friend.

⟫ YOUR ROBOT SIDEKICK IS
CUE.

Created by Toyota, Cue can't really run, but it can dribble and can shoot a basket with 100 percent accuracy.

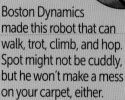

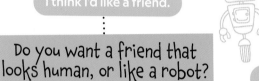

I want a sidekick that cooks for me.

» YOUR ROBOT SIDEKICK IS CAFE X.

This robot doesn't have a lot of personality, but it will make your coffee for you.

A cup of coffee, or a whole meal?

Coffee

A gourmet meal

My family

What do you want to help your family do?

» YOUR ROBOT SIDEKICK IS MOLEY ROBOTIC KITCHEN.

Moley's makers claim this robot cooks as well as any professional chef. Even more amazing: Moley cleans up after itself!

Everyday things

» YOUR ROBOT SIDEKICK IS BOT CARE.

This small bot from Samsung can remind you to take your medicine and monitor your heart rate. And if there's an emergency, Bot Care can phone for help.

Do you want a cute sidekick?

Sure!

I don't care what my sidekick looks like.

» YOUR ROBOT SIDEKICK IS BUDDY.

Small, huggable Buddy can do everything from guarding your home to helping you come up with recipes for dinner.

» YOUR ROBOT SIDEKICK IS GITA.

This robot looks like a big blue wheel. When you go to the store, Gita will follow you and carry your bags so you don't have to.

COULD YOU HAVE SURVIVED THE MIDDLE AGES?

F or many people, especially peasants, the Middle Ages (A.D. 500 to 1500) was a difficult time to be alive in Europe. Peasants tended to other people's land for little to no money. Count each statement you agree with to find out how you would have fared as a peasant in a medieval European village.

- I don't mind being told what to do.
- I like working outside in the sun.

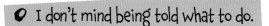

- I wouldn't mind sharing my room with a cow or a goat.
- Who needs personal space? I don't have to have privacy.
- When I'm hungry, nothing satisfies like a big plate of cabbage.
- I don't like going to school.
- I don't need art to be happy.
- I'd rather watch a live play than a movie on a screen.
- Windows in a house are nice, but I could live without them.

- I don't care much about books.
- Going to a crowded marketplace sounds like fun.
- I enjoy waking up early and going to bed early.
- I know how to make my own clothes.
- I know how to take care of farm animals.
- Clothes should be practical, not fashionable.
- My favorite sport is wrestling.
- I don't usually have a big appetite.

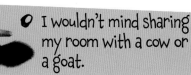
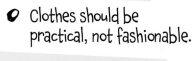

- Who needs a rug when you can spread straw on your floor?

- I really like tent camping.

- Vacations are overrated.

- Every year I plant vegetables in the garden.

- I'm not afraid of wolves.

- I don't usually shower every day.

- I'm strong.

- A mattress full of bedbugs wouldn't bug me.

- I enjoy being around chickens.

- I don't need a lot of money to be happy.

- Modern conveniences like air-conditioning aren't a "must" for me.

- I work well with others.

- I like making tools to solve problems.

A peasant's dinner in medieval times might be pottage stew, a dish made of vegetables and grains.

IF YOU COUNTED ...

1–10 Bubbles
You are thoroughly MODERN.

Living like a medieval peasant has no appeal for you. You'd rather work at a computer than do physical labor outdoors. Privacy is important to you, and you don't want anyone telling you what to wear or what you have to do with your life. And you're glad that you were taught how to read, so you can read about medieval times instead of living in them.

11–20 Bubbles
You'd visit, but not STAY THERE.

You enjoy being outdoors and have some basic farming or sewing skills that would serve you well in the Middle Ages. As a peasant, you'd spend most of your days working on the land, doing chores, and learning how to spin and weave fabric, and sew clothing. And while these things don't scare you, you like days off, time with your friends, and takeout pizza too much to be truly comfortable in medieval times.

21–30 Bubbles
You'd master the MIDDLE AGES!

Work outdoors and eat mostly vegetables? That sounds good to you! Work as a peasant could be incredibly tough, but there was also time to enjoy some of life's simple pleasures. In your free time, according to historians, you might go to plays and wrestle with your friends. You'd sleep comfortably on a buggy straw mattress in the same room as your family, with goats, sheep, and a cow just a few feet away.

WHAT'S YOUR CREATIVE STRENGTH?

When you hear the word "creative," you might think of a great artist like Vincent van Gogh or singer like Beyoncé. But you don't have to be famous to be creative. Answer these questions to find out your creative strength.

1. **A day at the beach! What do you do?**
   a. I create a beach scavenger hunt for my friends.
   b. I sketch plans for a machine that cleans trash out of the ocean.
   c. I build a sandcastle.
   d. I set up a lemonade stand.
   e. I start a game of beach volleyball.

2. **You're hungry, and you want cookies. What do you do?**
   a. I call my friends and ask them to come over with cookies.
   b. I start thinking about opening a cookie business.
   c. I bake some cookies.
   d. I smash cookies into crumbs and sprinkle them on ice cream.
   e. I go to the store and buy cookies.

3. **When you hear your favorite song, you ...**
   a. wonder how it would sound on a ukulele.
   b. imagine myself on stage, singing in front of a crowd.
   c. make a video of myself dancing to it.
   d. turn up the volume as loud as it goes.
   e. sing along.

4. **When you hear the word "dragon," you think ...**
   a. Has anyone ever made a robot dragon?
   b. I wish dragons were real!
   c. I love sculpting dragons out of clay.
   d. "Dragon" spelled backward is "NOGARD."
   e. I am going to write a poem about a dragon right now.

5. **Your school is putting on a play! What's your role?**
   a. I convince everyone to do the play outside.
   b. I design what the set will look like.
   c. I make the costumes.
   d. I get a starring role and don't stick to the script.
   e. I put out the call for auditions and sell the tickets.

6. **What happens when you take a walk through the woods?**
   a. I find a branch I can use as a walking stick.
   b. I get lost in my thoughts.
   c. I collect leaves and make a collage out of them.
   d. Why walk through the woods when you can dance?
   e. I download a trail map first and plan my route.

7. Make an amazing sandwich.

a. OK. How about peanut butter and pineapple slices on whole wheat?

b. Can I make it tomorrow? I'd like to dream up the perfect recipe.

c. Why just one? Can't I make a dozen?

d. I'll have peanut butter, ham, pickles, and potato chips on graham crackers.

e. How fast do you want it?

8. What does your town need right now?

a. a recycling plan for restaurant waste

b. a huge outdoor concert in the summer!

c. an arts center

d. fewer rules!

e. to turn that empty lot into a community garden

9. Plant a garden.

a. I'm going to try planting flowers in old tires.

b. I've got three different landscaping designs. I can't make up my mind!

c. Sure. Mine will grow all the ingredients you need to make pizza.

d. I'm going to plant jelly beans and see what comes up.

e. I already planted it!

10. You just adopted a dog!

a. I heard about a new training technique I'm going to try.

b. Maybe one day I'll run an animal shelter!

c. I baked him some yummy dog treats.

d. I'm going to train him to act like a cat.

e. I've already signed him up for obedience classes.

IF YOU CHOSE MOSTLY ...

A's ... Coming up with new ideas

You are an innovator, someone who can think of a solution that no one has thought of before—or maybe just a new way to wear your favorite scarf or a new game to play with your friends.

B's ... Coming up with big ideas

You are a dreamer, someone who loves to imagine how something could be bigger or better. You want to work for a brighter future for the world. Sometimes, though, you need help planning out your ideas or making them happen..

C's ... Making stuff

You are happiest when you are creating something with your hands, whether it's baking a cake, painting a picture, or building a birdhouse.

D's ... Breaking the rules

You're a renegade, someone who likes to experiment with different ways of doing things. You are often better working alone than on a team.

E's ... Taking action

Forget about sticking your toe into the pool—you dive right in! Sometimes you take action without planning carefully, but usually your friends appreciate you for always volunteering to get the job done.

FLOW-CHART
WHAT'S YOUR HISTORICAL LEADERSHIP STYLE?

What should a leader do?

Make life better for their citizens

Protect the empire

Do children make good rulers?

Sure, why not?

What is a skill that every leader should have?

What is a skill that every leader should have?

I don't think so.

The ability to communicate clearly

≫ YOU'D LEAD LIKE QUEEN ELIZABETH I.

Diplomatic skills

An open mind

≫ YOU'D LEAD LIKE SHUNZHI.

You value maturity, and this monarch is a good example of that. Elizabeth I was 25 when she claimed the throne of England. She inherited a war with France and a country divided by religious tension, but Elizabeth worked toward stability and unity, ushering in England's Golden Age.

≫ YOU'D LEAD LIKE KING TUT.

You'd probably admire the peacemaking skills of Egypt's boy king, who was nine years old when he took the throne of Egypt in 1332 B.C. He ruled for only 10 years before his death, but in that time he reversed a religious policy of his father's that had divided the kingdom.

In 1643, a five-year-old boy named Fulin became Shunzhi, the first emperor of China's Qing dynasty. Your objective nature is like this emperor's, who valued science, astronomy, and religious tolerance.

Expand the empire!

What skills does a conqueror need?

A passion for justice

Good planning

»YOU'D LEAD LIKE ATHELSTAN.

You share a spirit of fairness with this king. When he rose to the throne in 925, England was fighting with the Vikings. Athelstan used military skill to protect England while encouraging learning and justice in his court.

»YOU'D LEAD LIKE SAMMU-RAMAT.

This queen founded the city of Babylon in Assyria, in the ninth century B.C. Your organized nature might appreciate that she was known for the great building projects she planned, including canals, bridges, and roads over mountains.

A magnetic personality

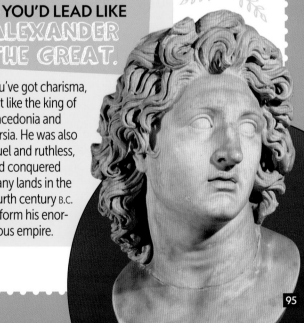

»YOU'D LEAD LIKE ALEXANDER THE GREAT.

You've got charisma, just like the king of Macedonia and Persia. He was also cruel and ruthless, and conquered many lands in the fourth century B.C. to form his enormous empire.

»YOU'D LEAD LIKE CLEOPATRA VII.

You know language is the key to communication, and this famous Egyptian ruler is thought to have spoken several of them! After taking the throne in 51 B.C., she forged strategic alliances in the Roman Empire to protect her land.

ARE YOU *Magical* OR *Practical?*

Do you ride through life on a winged horse—or walk through it wearing sensible shoes? To find out, decide if each statement below is true or false, and keep track of your answers.

TRUE OR FALSE

I'd be excited to find a four-leaf clover because they're good luck.

I write down my dreams so I'll remember them.

I knock on wood when I want to ward off bad luck.

Sometimes I have trouble making decisions.

I get bored easily.

I never take a test at school without my good-luck pencil.

A dragon would make a great pet.

If I had one wish, I would wish that I had wings.

I rarely read nonfiction books.

TRUE OR FALSE

I believe in magic.

When I see a star in the night sky, I make a wish.

I don't plan much; I just trust that everything will work out.

My favorite color is rainbow.

I stay inside every Friday the 13th.

I never use a map. I just follow the road and see where it goes.

If I were an animal, I would be a unicorn.

One day I'd like to search for the pot of gold at the end of a rainbow.

I would never spend the night alone in a haunted house.

I know my zodiac sign.

You can never have too much glitter.

I cry during movies a lot.

I wish my cat could talk.

Sometimes, I get lost in my daydreams.

I'm pretty sure I saw a ghost once.

My friends don't usually ask for my advice.

If you keep your eyes open, you can find magic anywhere you look.

Good things will happen to you if you just believe that they will.

I want to live in a castle someday.

Having dreams is more important than setting goals.

I can live without a schedule.

IF YOU CHOSE MOSTLY ...

True... You're *Magical!*

You love to read books about dragons and fairies, and these books help fuel your big imagination. You believe that there is magic all around you if you just look for it. You're also superstitious—just like many professional athletes. Michael Jordan, for example, always wore specific shorts under his uniform when he played to bring him luck. Some psychologists think superstitions like these might actually work because they give athletes a boost of confidence.

False ... You're *Practical!*

Your friends know that you are someone they can count on—you're always on time and always know what to do when something goes wrong. You'd rather read a biography of an athlete or a book about animal habitats than a fairy tale. You think superstitions are silly, and you definitely don't believe in ghosts. And you gain confidence by knowing that you've taken the steps you need to achieve your goals.

WHAT'S YOUR PREY POWER?

Are you a trickster?
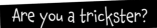

Yes, I love to prank people!

I don't fool around. I'm more dangerous than I look.

How about charades? Are you good at that game?

No, I'm not good at charades.

What makes you dangerous?

Yes, I'm a great actor!

What do you do when you're scared?

›› YOU'RE A MIMIC OCTOPUS.

This Indonesian octopus has great acting skills, too—it can change the color and texture of its skin to look like a creature that its predator fears, and scare it away.

I freeze up!

I run away!

›› YOU'RE A VIRGINIA OPOSSUM!

Freezing up in a dangerous situation works for this opossum, which "plays dead" to trick predators such as coyotes. It falls into a comatose-like state and emits a liquid that smells like a dead opossum to the coyote.

›› YOU'RE A FIVE-LINED SKINK!

You're a runner, but this lizard has an extra trick that you don't: It can detach part or all of its tail, which keeps wiggling like a snake and distracts the predator while the skink runs away.

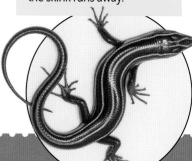

I'm not sure if I'm a trickster, but I do like to surprise my friends.

Do you think it's better to protect yourself or protect others?

Poison

» YOU'RE A
BOMBARDIER BEETLE.

If this beetle is attacked by a predator, it heats up. The beetle mixes two substances inside its body until they reach boiling temperature and then shoots them out of its abdomen.

Protect myself

» YOU'RE A
POISON DART FROG.

These tiny, colorful frogs eat ants that contain organic chemicals called alkaloids. These are stored in the frogs' bodies. The alkaloids then turn into poison strong enough to kill most animals almost instantly.

Protect others

Slime

» YOU'RE A
HAGFISH!

When this tube-shaped fish is threatened by a predator such as a harbor seal, it oozes slime from its pores. Any animal trying to bite the fish gets a suffocating mouthful of slime and clogged gills instead.

» YOU'RE A
MALAYSIAN EXPLODING ANT.

If the ant colony is under attack, one ant will contract its muscles and burst glands full of a toxic liquid, spraying the sticky substance over the attackers. This ant dies, but the colony is safe.

ARE YOU A
PERFECTIONIST?

Are you the kind of person who wants to flow through life flawlessly? Count each statement you agree with to find out!

- My school locker is neatly organized.

- To reach your dreams, you need to work hard.

- If I make a mistake, I can't stop thinking about it.

- I'd rather be the president than the vice president.

- I don't like to eat cookies because crumbs are too messy.

- I always color inside the lines.

- I put off doing things until I know I can do them right.

- I like to set goals for myself.

- If I burn a slice of toast, I throw it away.

- I would never wear a wrinkly shirt.

- Why go for an A when you can go for an A+?

- If I compete and don't come in first place, I've failed.

- I organize my clothes by color.

- Everybody needs to follow the rules.

- It's important to always work toward your goals.

- When I'm in a group, I like to be the leader.

- If I want something done right, I do it myself.

- Something is either right or wrong; there is no in-between.

- It feels great to be praised when you do a good job.
- I think I would enjoy a career in accounting.

- One of the scariest things I can think of is failing at something.
- If I see one of my friends making a mistake, I correct them.
- If I spill food on my shirt, I change it right away.
- It doesn't matter if you've done your best if you don't succeed.
- I love having autocorrect on my phone.

- I do my own laundry.
- I always use an alarm to wake me up.
- I hate being wrong.

- I get a haircut once every six weeks.
- I make my bed every morning.

IF YOU COUNTED ...

1–10 Bubbles

You might be pretty RELAXED.

You believe that everybody makes mistakes, and that's OK—mistakes are part of life! You don't mind getting messy, and if ice cream drips on your shirt you'll just wipe it off and keep enjoying your food. This idea of "going with the flow" echoes the ancient Chinese philosophy of Taoism, which teaches that humans need to live in harmony with the natural order of things.

11–20 Bubbles

You've got an eye FOR DETAIL.

Competition energizes you! You're happy playing team sports or running for class president. If you lose, it doesn't bother you too much. As long as you know you did your best, you're OK. If you are the leader of a group, you give everyone a job, and if somebody fails, you don't give them a hard time. And you don't give yourself a hard time, either, which means you're basically a happy person.

21–30 Bubbles

You're probably a PERFECTIONIST.

The world needs perfectionists, people who pay attention to detail and are careful not to make mistakes. Perfectionists bake showstopping pastries and write code that shoots rockets into space. If you're a perfectionist, you might put pressure on yourself to always win and succeed, so try to relax! Remind yourself that it's OK to make mistakes, and remember that you can learn a lot by trying something new, even if you fail in the end.

WHICH AWESOME SPORT SHOULD YOU TRY?

You might have played baseball and soccer, but there are some sports out there that you may never have heard of! Which one might be a good one to try? Keep track of your answers to find out.

1. **Which popular sport do you enjoy most?**
   a. handball
   b. soccer
   c. golf
   d. hockey

2. **Pick a mascot:**
   a. alligator
   b. tiger
   c. leopard
   d. octopus

3. **Which piece of playground equipment do you like most?**
   a. the spinner
   b. the climbing tower
   c. the bouncy car
   d. the rope bridge

4. **Why do you play sports?**
   a. I'm very competitive.
   b. I like to push myself.
   c. I like to have fun.
   d. I want to keep fit.

5. **Which of these words best describes you?**
   a. fast
   b. intelligent
   c. loud
   d. focused

6. **Pick a fruit:**
   a. pomegranate
   b. papaya
   c. dragon fruit
   d. strawberry

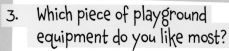
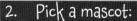
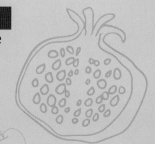
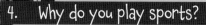

7. Which of these activities do you like to do with friends?

    a. watch the World Cup on TV

    b. play kickball

    c. go bike riding

    d. go to the pool

8. Pick a color:

    a. green

    b. red

    c. black

    d. blue

9. Pick something to wear while you're playing:

    a. elbow pads

    b. shorts

    c. helmet

    d. swim flippers

10. How active are you?

    a. Very. I'm always moving.

    b. I like to keep in shape.

    c. I'd rather take the bus than walk.

    d. I move a lot, cleaning or working outside.

IF YOU CHOSE MOSTLY ...

A's ... You should try jai alai.

You're physically active and love to keep moving, which is why you might enjoy this fast-paced game that originated in Europe's Basque region. Athletes use a scoop strapped to their arm to bounce a ball off the walls in a three-walled court. The scoop, called a cesta, allows the player to hurl the hard rubber ball, or pelota, at superfast speeds. Today, it's most popular in Spain, Mexico, and the U.S. state of Florida.

B's ... You should try Sepak Takraw.

You want a challenging sport that requires quick thinking, and this one might be for you. This combo of volleyball and soccer has been played formally in Malaysia since the 1940s. The game is set up like volleyball, with players on either side of a net, but there's a catch— like in soccer, you can't touch the ball with your hands!

C's ... You should try tuk tuk polo.

If playing a sport on wheels sounds perfect to you, then you might like tuk tuk polo, a game from Sri Lanka. Traditional polo is played on horseback, and riders with long mallets try to hit a ball into a goal. This sport is played on tuk tuks— small three-wheeled vehicles normally used as taxis. Each tuk tuk holds two players—one to drive, and one to swing the mallet. (Maybe wait until you're old enough to drive to try this one!)

D's ... You should try octopush.

You love the water, which is why this underwater, hockey-like game might be for you. Players wear a mask, snorkel, and flippers in a swimming pool and try to push a puck across the floor of the pool using a stick. The sport was invented in England in the 1950s by underwater divers who wanted a more interesting way to get fit than swimming laps.

WHICH **SUPERCUTE MAMMAL** ARE YOU?

What do you like to eat?

I'm not picky.

I prefer vegetarian meals.

Do you nap during the day?

No, I'm very active during the day.

Would you rather spend a day in the woods or at the beach?

Yes. I have a lot of energy at night.

Do you like crowds?

Yes, the more the merrier!

Are you good at climbing trees?

Nope, I avoid them.

I'm a great climber!

I'd rather stay on the ground, thanks.

» YOU'RE A HARRIS'S ANTELOPE SQUIRREL.

Scientists aren't sure how this solitary squirrel, which burrows in the rocky deserts of North America, manages to dine on cactus fruit without being injured by the sharp spines.

» YOU'RE A RED PANDA.

This Asian animal is about the size of a house cat and is known for its beautiful bushy reddish brown fur.

» YOU'RE A FENNEC FOX.

This desert-dwelling animal searches for food at night, when it's cooler. Its big ears also help it stay cool by radiating body heat—and make it look cute to boot!

I'm a meat lover.

Are you more cute or fierce?

In the woods

»YOU'RE A CHEVROTAIN.

This animal is also called a mouse deer, but it's neither mouse nor deer. It belongs to a family of hoofed mammals that munch on forest plants at night.

Definitely more cute!

»YOU'RE A MARGAY.

This "tiger cat" from Central and South America is a predator, but it feeds mostly on small birds, frogs, and insects.

At the beach

»YOU'RE A QUOKKA.

A Dutch explorer mistook this cutie for a giant rat and named its island Rotte Nest (which means "rat's nest"). These creatures are a type of wallaby, and they dine on grasses and shrubs.

I've got a fierce streak.

Which do you like better, summer or winter?

»YOU'RE A SERVAL.

This African cat hunts for small mammals such as rodents and hares. Its extra-long legs help it pounce on prey—and also explain its nickname, "giraffe cat."

Summer   Winter

»YOU'RE A JAPANESE WEASEL.

This weasel's white winter coat might make it look like an adorable plushie, but watch out! This expert hunter will chase after prey day and night on all kinds of terrain.

»YOU'RE A MEERKAT.

Meerkats live in large packs in warrens dug under the African savanna. During the day, they search for insects, spiders, scorpions, and other small animals to eat.

WHAT'S YOUR ROLE ON MARS?

THE YEAR IS 2123, AND YOU AND YOUR FAMILY LIVE IN A SETTLEMENT ON MARS. WHEN YOU'RE NOT AT SCHOOL, YOU HELP WITH THE TASKS OF RUNNING THE COLONY. SOON YOU'LL TRAIN WITH ONE OF THE SPECIALTY DIVISIONS THAT WORKS 24/7 TO HELP HUMANS ON MARS STAY ALIVE—AND THRIVE. YOU HAVE TO DECIDE WHAT YOU WANT TO DO, BUT YOU'RE NOT SURE YET. TAKE THIS QUIZ TO HELP YOU CHOOSE HOW YOU WANT TO SPEND YOUR FUTURE ON THE RED PLANET.

1. It's Saturday morning on Mars, and your alarm goes off at 6 a.m. What's your first thought?

a. I wish this bed was more comfortable.

b. I'm hungry!

c. I hope Mom takes me on that crater expedition with her.

d. I'm so excited! The supply ship is coming today!

2. What holographic image is projected on your bedroom wall?

a. an aerial view of the colony

b. a flower

c. the two moons of Mars

d. Earth's biggest pop star

3. Do you use a calendar app to plan your day?

a. Of course! I plan every day down to the minute.

b. I plan *some* things, but not everything.

c. I like to see where each day takes me.

d. I use it to plan things with my friends.

4. You live in an underground settlement with 50 other families and with shared spaces. Which idea do you have to improve the cafeteria experience?

a. It should be open 24/7 for workers on the night shift.

b. I'd like the meals to have more fresh veggies.

c. None. I prefer protein bars on the go.

d. There should be longer tables so everyone can eat together.

5. It's almost time for the supply ship to arrive. You make your way through the tunnels to the colony's loading bay. Why are you there?

- **a.** I've heard a new colony might be built, and I want to find out if it's true.
- **b.** To find out if any new plant seeds are in the shipment.
- **c.** I want to help if anything goes wrong.
- **d.** I am part of the official welcoming committee.

6. It's time for your morning exercise. What do you want to do?

- **a.** shoot hoops in the newly installed basketball court
- **b.** jog through the hallways of the settlement
- **c.** practice rappelling on the indoor climbing wall
- **d.** exercise with a group class in the activity room

7. What do you do on your device while you wait?

- **a.** look up a recipe
- **b.** take care of a virtual pet
- **c.** play a word search game
- **d.** learn a new language

8. There are space tourists on the supply ship, and one is your age. The hospitality captain asks you to give the kid a tour. Where do you start?

- **a.** I show off my cool room.
- **b.** I want to show off the tomatoes I helped grow.
- **c.** I go to the vehicle bay, where I'm building a dirt bike.
- **d.** I go to the cafeteria for a smoothie and ask the visitor lots of questions about life on Earth.

9. "This place is so cool. Do you ever want to leave the settlement?" the Earth visitor asks. What do you answer?

- **a.** "No, Mars is my home."
- **b.** "I'd like to go to an Earth jungle."
- **c.** "Yes! I'd love to explore the whole universe someday."
- **d.** "I'd love to go to the city on Earth where my parents were born."

10. The visitors have brought items for the Earth museum on Mars. Which are you most excited about?

- **a.** a board game
- **b.** flower seeds
- **c.** a piece of a spacecraft that landed on Earth's moon
- **d.** walkie-talkies

Continued ...

11. That night, the colony gathers in the cafeteria to watch a movie. What kind do you hope it will be?

- **a.** a mystery
- **b.** a documentary
- **c.** science fiction
- **d.** a comedy

12. The next day, the visitor goes to your school classes with you. Which subject is your favorite?

- **a.** geology
- **b.** biology
- **c.** astronomy
- **d.** Earth history

13. It's time to take your visitor to the planet's surface. You both put on your space suits. Where do you go?

- **a.** to explore a giant crater
- **b.** to the rock quarry
- **c.** to the vehicle bay to check out the terrain rovers
- **d.** to the communications satellites

14. As you both head out, you see a cloud of red dust in the distance. It could be a dust storm coming. What do you do first?

- **a.** I remember protocol and radio for help with my comm device.
- **b.** I panic and forget what I'm supposed to do.
- **c.** I check a digital blueprint of the colony to find shelter nearby.
- **d.** I try to keep my visitor calm.

15. It's not a dust storm! It's a massive transport vehicle heading out to the location of the new colony. What do you do?

- **a.** I ask the team members on the transport about the new colony.
- **b.** I'm shaken up and want to go back to the underground settlement.
- **c.** I ask if I can go explore the new location.
- **d.** I take the visitor back to the settlement to watch a video about the dust storms.

16. After a busy day on the surface, you and your visitor relax. What do you do?

- **a.** We chill out and talk.
- **b.** We listen to music.
- **c.** We go to the observatory and look at the stars.
- **d.** I introduce the visitor to my friends.

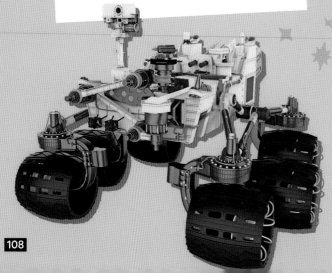

17. It's dinnertime. What Mars settlement specialty are you excited for your visitor to try?

    a. tofu and veggie stir-fry

    b. veggie noodles with tomato and kale sauce

    c. sweet-and-sour tempeh

    d. coconut ice cream

18. At the end of the day, your visitor tells you, "We have a lot in common. We're both _____ people."

    a. curious

    b. quiet

    c. fearless

    d. friendly

19. Your visitor's family is thinking about joining the new colony. They ask you, "What do you like best about living on Mars?" You answer:

    a. "The habitat is really comfortable."

    b. "Watching the plants grow in the greenhouse is nice."

    c. "There's always something new to explore."

    d. "The people are awesome."

20. It's time to apply to a specialty team. You're still not sure what you want to do, but you know that you want to ...

    a. solve problems.

    b. work in an indoor environment.

    c. be on the surface a lot.

    d. work with a lot of people.

IF YOU CHOSE MOSTLY ...

A's ... You're on the Habitat Team.

You like solving problems, and you're most excited about making comfortable spaces for the settlers. Because of dangerous radiation levels on Mars, habitats must be built either underground or built into natural features such as craters and cliffs. Habitat designers might create features like walls with computer screens built in that are hooked up to outside cameras—the next best thing to a window!

B's ... You're on the Greenhouse Team.

You're a nurturing, patient person who loves plants. On Mars, the settlement will rely on plants to survive. They'll have to be grown with seeds brought from Earth and nutrients taken from rocks on Mars. Besides providing food, plants will also produce extra oxygen in the settlement's  living spaces. As a member of this team, you'll be busy tending to some of the most important living things in the settlement.

C's ... You're on the Exploration Team.

You love to discover new things, and on Mars there is plenty to explore. To keep the settlement going, you'll need to find sources of ice to provide water, and rocks with nutrients that can be broken down to feed plants. You'll search the planet for those resources as well as sites to build new habitats.

D's ... You're on the Earth Collaboration Team.

You are a people person, and that quality makes you a good fit for this team, which coordinates all dealings with Earth. While your colony is very self-sufficient, there are still things you need from your home planet, including medi-  cines, metals such as gold and silver, and the robots that help with building and maintaining the settlement.

INDEX

Boldface indicates illustrations.

A

Adventurousness 14–15
Amazon rainforest 54–57
Ancient civilizations 66–67,
94–95
Animal careers 86–87, **87**
Animals
Australian 64–65, **64–65**
creepy-crawly 12–13,
12–13
oddball 48–49, **48–49**
prey 98–99, **98–99**
stinky 82–83, **82–83**
supercute 104–105, **104–105**
see also Birds of prey; Pets;
Reptiles
Artistic spirit 50–51

B

Birds of prey 22–23, **22–23**
Bugs 12–13, **12–13**

C

Careers
animal 86–87, **87**
ocean 62–63, **62–63**
planet-protecting 34–35
Cats
as pets 37
vs. dogs 26–27
Cities 16–17, **16–17**
Creative strengths 92–93
Curiosity 84–85

D

Desserts 18–19, **18–19**
Dinosaurs 58–59, **58–59**
Dogs
as pets 37
vs. cats 26–27

E

Early birds 68–69, **69**
Earth (planet): protecting
34–35, 81
Edison, Thomas 78–79, **79**
Expeditions 54–57, 70–71
Extroverts 52–53

F

Fame 80–81
Fashion, historical 32–33,
32–33
Feeling vs. thinking 44–45
Friends, kinds of 74–75

G

Galactic personalities 24–25
Gemstones 76–77, **76–77**
Greece, ancient
fashion 33, **33**
gods **46**, 47, **47**
life in 67

I

Insects 12–13, **12–13**
Introverts 52–53
Islands, deserted **60**, 60–61

D

Desserts 18–19, **18–19**

L

Leadership styles 94–95

M

Magic 96–97
Mars (planet) 106–109
Middle Ages 90–91
Mountain climbing 10–11, 14,
14
Mythical creatures 30–31,
30–31

N

Natural wonders 70–71, **70–71**
Night owls 68–69, **69**

O

Ocean careers 62–63, **62–63**
Oddball animals 48–49,
48–49
Outgoingness 52–53

P

Perfectionism 100–101
Pets 36–37, **36–37**; *see also*
Cats; Dogs
Pirates 28–29, 41
Planet-protecting careers
34–35
Planning 38–39
Practicalness 18, 96–97
Prey animals 98–99, **98–99**

R

Reptiles 42–43, **42–43;**
 see also Dinosaurs
Risk taking 14–15
Robot sidekicks 88–89, **88–89**
Rules: making and breaking
 20–21, 93

S

Sci-fi characters **40**, 40–41, **41**
Seriousness 72–73
Shark superpowers 8–9

Shyness 52–53
Silliness 72–73
Space
 galactic personalities 24–25
 Martian colony 106–109
 sci-fi characters 40–41
Spontaneity 38–39
Sports 102–103, **102–103**
Stinky animals 82–83, **82–83**
Supercute mammals
 104–105, **104–105**
Survival
 deserted island 60–61
 Middle Ages 90–91

T

Tesla, Nikola 78–79, **79**
Thinking vs. feeling 44–45
Thrill seeking 14–15
Tricksters 98–99

PHOTO CREDITS

NATIONAL GEOGRAPHIC and Yellow Border Design are trademarks of the National Geographic Society, used under license.

Since 1888, the National Geographic Society has funded more than 14,000 research, conservation, education, and storytelling projects around the world. National Geographic Partners distributes a portion of the funds it receives from your purchase to National Geographic Society to support programs including the conservation of animals and their habitats. To learn more, visit natgeo.com/info.

For more information, visit nationalgeographic.com, call 1-877-873-6846, or write to the following address:

National Geographic Partners, LLC
1145 17th Street NW
Washington, DC 20036-4688 U.S.A.

For librarians and teachers: nationalgeographic.com/books/librarians-and-educators

More for kids from National Geographic: natgeokids.com

National Geographic Kids magazine inspires children to explore their world with fun yet educational articles on animals, science, nature, and more. Using fresh storytelling and amazing photography, *Nat Geo Kids* shows kids ages 6 to 14 the fascinating truth about the world—and why they should care. natgeo.com/subscribe

For rights or permissions inquiries, please contact National Geographic Books Subsidiary Rights: bookrights@natgeo.com

Designed by Fuszion

Trade paperback ISBN: 978-1-4263-7317-6
Reinforced library binding ISBN: 978-1-4263-7594-1

The publisher would like to thank the book team: Kathryn Williams and Rose Davidson, editors; Sanjida Rashid, art director; Sarah J. Mock, senior photo editor; Mahnoor Ali, researcher; and Gus Tello, designer.

Printed in China
23/RRDH/1